PHARMA CUSTOMER EXPERIENCE

Se M'Dale

12/27/21

12/27/51

PHARMA CUSTOMER EXPERIENCE

20 SECRETS TO 10X YOUR CX AND BOOST PATIENT OUTCOMES

SEAN McDADE, PhD

LIONCREST
PUBLISHING

PHARMA CUSTOMER EXPERIENCE

20 Secrets to 10X Your CX & Boost Patient Outcomes

ISBN   978-1-5445-2561-7   *Hardcover*

   978-1-5445-2559-4   *Paperback*

   978-1-5445-2560-0   *Ebook*

   978-1-5445-2562-4   *Audiobook*

The book is dedicated to the people who work in pharmaceutical and biotechnology companies. They are now the heroes to the world as they help us get past the COVID-19 pandemic. Yet, for decades they have helped people live better and long lives. Heroes now and always, thank you for everything you do!

CONTENTS

INTRODUCTION

More than once, pharma has literally saved the world. As I write this in July 2021, there have been three vaccines approved in the US for COVID-19, one by Pfizer, one by Moderna, and one by Johnson & Johnson.

Another COVID-19 vaccine, this one by AstraZeneca (and Oxford), has been approved in the UK. And there are several more vaccines on the horizon that will help the world get past this pandemic.

Each is doing their part to let us feel hopeful again. Hugging a parent? Going to a ball game with friends? Seeing your favorite band in concert? Yes, yes, and yes!

Pharma is making all of it possible. They should be heroes to the world! And yet, most people are indifferent at best. It's not that pharma companies are faceless brands that consumers can't connect with as they do with Apple, Spotify, and Peloton. But according to The Harris poll, only 53% of consumers hold a positive view of pharma.

And a recent Gallup poll on consumer perceptions found pharma rated *below* electric utilities and oil and gas!

But why?

Because pharma does not emotionally connect with its ultimate customer, the patient, like great consumer brands do. Let me explain.

The best consumer brands are completely obsessed with the customer experience, and the entire company is focused on it. These companies first create each customer experience with intention. Nothing is left to chance. They meticulously map every aspect of the customer experience—from first engagement to first purchase to continued usage over time.

And everything in between.

Everything.

The great consumer brands emotionally connect with the customer. Over and over again.

And they do that by delivering experiences that customers value, remember, and share with others.

Pharma does not do this. At least not consistently.

But they can. And, more importantly, they must if they want to continue to thrive. Patients who have positive experiences with pharma are more likely to join clinical trials, successfully onboard to new medications, adhere over time, and enjoy positive medical outcomes.

And better experiences provide pharma with the opportunity to connect with underserved populations and help the people in those populations live longer, better quality lives. Put another way, a great patient experience means *all* people have a chance at better medical outcomes and better lives.

Why am I qualified to write about this topic?

The company I founded in 2001, PeopleMetrics, has been working with pharma companies since we started. We have helped pharma understand stakeholders' needs, wants, and experiences.

Up until 2015, most of this work was traditional market research type work, primarily with physicians and other Healthcare Professionals (HCPs)—sales force effectiveness, market landscape, segmentation, message testing, you name it.

And then in 2015, we got a call from a client who asked us

if we had measured the experience with "patient support services"? We asked, "What in the world are patient support services?"

We learned quickly. Patient support services, also known as "patient support programs (PSPs)," are game changers for patients. These services help patients with access to their medication, improve adherence, better manage their disease, reduce complications, provide financial assistance, and more.

Then in 2017, a client asked us if we could help them measure the patient experience in a global clinical trial. This was new and incredibly exciting territory. A better patient experience in clinical trials impacts the ability to recruit and retain patients (including those from underserved populations), informs design for future trials, and provides an indication to the effectiveness of different trial sites.

We started to understand that being patient-centric applied across commercial *and* clinical.

Hmmm.

At the same time, the customer experience (CX) space was exploding, with nearly every industry embracing the concept and investing heavily to better engage with their customers. There even appeared a new category of software called "experience management," which helps companies measure and manage the customer experience. Analysts like Forrester and Gartner cover this space regularly.

This got us thinking, how does customer experience, or CX as we call it, apply to pharma?

And "pharma CX" was born.

In 2018, I wrote a book entitled *Listen or Die: 40 Lessons that Turn Customer Feedback into Gold.* I wrote that book because customer feedback about their experiences is the foundation for emotional connection between companies and customers.

Indeed, customer experience remains the only true differentiator in most industries.

Yes, even in pharma. Especially in pharma.

This is easily the most important work my company has done or will do.

It is one thing helping a hotel measure and improve the checkout experience or helping a telecom company improve their customer support.

But it's quite another to help a pharma company make it

easier for a new patient who has cancer to get the treatment they need to live a longer and higher-quality life. Or help a pharma company recruit and retain patients for a clinical trial that results in a new medicine that saves lives that can't be saved today.

So, we got to work.

This book is about mindset more than anything else. Specifically, it's about pharma changing its mindset from one focused on developing products to one focused on delivering experiences. I want to shift pharma's approach to model the companies that cultivate not just customers, but advocates and raving fans, over and over again.

I am writing this book to share twenty secrets that my company, PeopleMetrics, has learned in helping pharma companies focus on the customer and create exceptional experiences. Each secret falls within one of four sections.

The first section introduces three secrets that lay the foundation for pharma CX. The second offers four secrets that introduce how pharma CX applies to both clinical and commercial teams. The third section contains ten secrets around patient support services, the front-line for commercial pharma CX. The final section includes three secrets that are key to implementing a successful pharma CX program.

And at the end of the book, there is a bonus section, which takes a peek into the future.

Let's dig in.

PHARMA CX FUNDAMENTALS

SECRET
#1

BE OBSESSED

Every pharma company claims to be patient-centric, but those who are truly patient-obsessed always create, measure, and manage customer experiences.

If you read almost any pharma company mission statement, you will undoubtedly see patients or "patient-centricity" mentioned prominently. Or referenced with terms such as "people," "individual," "lives," "life changing," or "health."

Take a look at the mission statements from the top pharma companies in the table below. Almost all of them refer in some way to improving the lives of patients. How could these companies *not* be considered patient-centric?

Company Name	Mission Statement
Pfizer	At Pfizer, we innovate every day to make the world a healthier place. It was the vision of Charles Pfizer at the very beginning, and it holds true today in everything we do. From scientific discovery to breakthrough products to our essential partnerships around the world, we're committed to quality healthcare for *everyone*. Because every *individual* matters.
Roche	Doing what *patients* need next.
Novartis	Our mission is to discover new ways to improve and extend *people's* lives.
Johnson & Johnson	Our credo stems from a belief that *consumers*, employees, and the community are all equally important.
Merck & Co.	We share one vision and one mission: to save and improve *lives*.
Sanofi	Every day, Sanofi's 100,000 employees are committed to improve the *lives of people* around the world, with sustainable and responsible solutions and initiatives.
AbbVie	Create an innovation-driven, *patient-focused* specialty biopharmaceutical company capable of achieving sustainable top-tier performance through outstanding execution and a consistent stream of innovative new medicines.
GlaxoSmithKline	A science-led global healthcare company with a special purpose: to help *people* do more, feel better, live longer.
Amgen	To serve *patients*.
Gilead Sciences	To discover, develop, and commercialize innovative therapeutics in the areas of unmet medical needs that improve *patient* care.
Bristol Myers Squibb	Bristol Myers Squibb is a global biopharmaceutical company whose mission is to discover, develop, and deliver innovative medicines that help *patients* prevail over serious diseases.
AstraZeneca	We push the boundaries of science to deliver *life-changing* medicines.

Company Name	Mission Statement
Eli Lilly	Lilly unites caring with discovery to create medicines that make life better for *people* around the world.
Bayer	Bayer: Science for a Better *Life*.
Novo Nordisk	We turn ideas into medicines for *people* living with serious chronic diseases.
Takeda	Our Mission is to strive toward better *health* and a Brighter Future for *people* worldwide through leading innovation in medicine.
Celgene	At Celgene, our mission is to discover, develop, and deliver innovative medicines that improve and extend *patients'* lives worldwide.
Boehringer Ingelheim	Since its founding, the privately held company has been committed to researching, developing, manufacturing, and marketing novel treatments for *human* and veterinary medicine.
Teva	Our mission is to be a global leader in generics and biopharmaceuticals, improving the lives of *patients* across the world.
Mylan	At Mylan, we are committed to setting new standards in healthcare. Working together around the world to provide 7 billion *people* access to high-quality medicine, we: innovate to satisfy unmet needs; make reliability and service excellence a habit; do what's right, not what's easy; impact the future through passionate global leadership.
CSL	We develop and deliver innovative biotherapies and influenza vaccines that save *lives* and help *people* with life-threatening medical conditions live full lives. We are driven by our deep passion to serve hundreds of thousands of patients and other stakeholders around the world.
Daichii Sankyo	To contribute to the enrichment of quality of *life* around the world through the creation of innovative pharmaceuticals and through the provision of pharmaceuticals addressing diverse medical needs.

Company Name	Mission Statement
Otsuka	Our mission is clear: Otsuka-people, creating new products for better *health* worldwide.
UCB	To transform *aging* by building a culture of community, wholeness, and peace.
Les Laboratoires Servier	We are committed to therapeutic progress to serve *patient* needs with the help of healthcare professionals. We strive to provide future generations with a world where quality healthcare is available and accessible to all.
Eisai	We give first thought to *patients* and their families, and to increasing the benefits healthcare provides.

(Emphases added.)

But what does patient-centricity really mean? That's less clear. Are all these companies really obsessed with delivering exceptional experiences to their customers? Probably not.

Isn't it enough to develop innovative, safe drugs that improve the quality and, in many cases, length of a patient's life?

No, not anymore.

Consider this example from one of our clients who is truly obsessed with the customer experience.

Plasma donations are used by pharmaceutical companies to make life-saving drugs that treat rare and chronic conditions. Creating a great experience for donors is key to having the consistent flow of plasma needed to bring these drugs to market.

Our client has a significant investment in plasma donation centers and experienced a decline in donor satisfaction scores.

The good news is that we had already implemented a continuous, real-time donor feedback program and were able to immediately uncover that the decline in donor satisfaction tied closely to the amount of time it took to get the donor into the scheduled appointment.

This finding was further supported by ample donor comments expressing frustration with long lines and unpleasant conditions while waiting.

Armed with this real-time customer feedback, our client created a new check-in system. This new process was not only more efficient, but also gave donors flexibility in the waiting process.

After making this change, our client noticed immediate improvement in their donor satisfaction scores and, in turn, plasma donation levels.

To summarize, our client *created* a customer experience, *continuously* measured customer feedback *in real-time*, and used that feedback to *proactively make a change* that dramatically improved the customer experience and, in turn, business outcomes. This obsession with the customer is ingrained in their culture, and they see the benefits of this mindset daily. Before I go any further, a fair warning that there is still a considerable amount of foundational content to cover in this chapter, which consequently is significantly longer than subsequent ones. All secrets that follow are based on the principles from this chapter.

WHAT IS PHARMA CX?

The key to patient-centricity is embracing what I call "pharma customer experience (CX)," or "pharma CX." Simply put, *pharma CX is in the act of intentionally creating, continuously measuring in real-time, and proactively managing the customer experience.*

When our client course-corrected the check-in process based on real-time feedback from donors, that was pharma CX in action.

But before I dive much further into pharma CX, it's worth asking: who are pharma's customers? Traditionally, they have been physicians who prescribe medications for patients. Now, the definition has expanded to include other HCPs (e.g., nurses, office coordinators, etc.), caregivers, as well as patients and even donors, as in the example above.

Two main trends have caused this shift in the customer make-up.

The first is that pharma has shifted from mass-market drugs to specialties. These specialty drugs now represent almost half the overall market (in terms of spend) and often require close interaction with patients. While specialty drugs were the first to adopt this close interaction with patients, this is a need that even mass-market drugs will have to satisfy as well.

The second trend is that the "consumerization" of health-care is upon us. Patients now are demanding and expecting more involvement in their own healthcare decisions. Patients expect to have support throughout their treatment journey and to access that support where and when they choose. Pharma is certainly investing in patient support programs (see Secret #9) to align with this trend. One could argue that pharma must support the patient in their health-care journey. Pharma knows best if these drugs work and how they can help patients achieve their medical outcomes.

The impact of these two trends has been an understanding of the patient as the main customer, and I will so consider the patient in this book. So, when I write "customer experience," I am primarily referring to the experiences of patients. However, many of the concepts discussed in this book can apply to both patients and the stakeholders who impact the patient experience throughout the treatment journey. Ultimately, it is up to each pharma company to determine their primary customer. However, if your mission statement focuses on the patient while most marketing dollars target physicians, it may be time to reconsider. At the very least, patients and HCPs should both be considered primary co-customers of pharma.

Now, let's unpack the three-part definition of pharma CX.

The first step is to be intentional about creating the customer experience. Customers engage with pharma constantly, from simple experiences like onboarding onto new medications or donating plasma, to larger ones like joining clinical trials and choosing which drug to prescribe. But how many of these include thoughtful or intentional emotional connections between pharma and their customers? Very few. For pharma to proactively create those connections is rarer still. Pharma tends to see customer experiences as unavoidable steps to get through, rather than chances to emotionally connect. In the plasma donation example, our client was determined to create the best experience possible for donors. They knew that a great donor experience was the key to obtaining the plasma necessary for developing life-saving medications. Like the best CX companies in other industries, this company maps out and creates each customer experience with intention. See Secret #3 on customer journey mapping for more on this important topic.

The second step is to implement a process by which you measure CX continuously and in real-time to understand its effectiveness. And don't just measure every once in a while! Measure *continuously* and *in real-time* at touchpoints that matter the most—often called "moments of truth." In the plasma donation example, our client determined that wait time was their "moment of truth" based on continuous and real-time feedback from their customers, and that this moment of truth was not going well and something had to be fixed immediately. See Secret #2 for more on how this type of pharma CX measurement differs from market research. And see Secret #3 on how to best identify "moments of truth."

In the third step, pharma must proactively manage CX. What does that look like? When a customer has a poor experience, there should be a process in place to follow up with that customer and resolve their issue. In the plasma donation example, the pharma company consistently followed up with donors who had bad experiences and then made a systemic change to improve donor experiences going forward!

Here's another example. One of our clients introduced a rare disease therapy that required infusions as part of treatment. This client followed the pharma CX process. First, they intentionally created the customer experience by providing field nurses to teach patients proper infusion techniques. Next, our client continuously measured the patient experience in real-time immediately after an interaction with a field nurse via an online survey. They learned that while patients appreciated the field nurses, many were still confused about the infusion process and needed more education. The pharma company took proactive action by having the field nurse immediately follow up with patients who indicated they were not comfortable with the administration of their new therapy and got them the educational resources they needed. The pharma CX process enabled this pharma company to tailor its services to the educational needs of each patient for a complex medication and increase onboarding, adherence, and ultimately medical outcomes for the patient.

I know what you are thinking. Yes, you will still have guardrails that protect PII (Personally Identifiable Information), but the act of individual customer follow-up has a major impact on successful CX (see Secret #17 for more). Managing customer experiences also means identifying key customer gaps or pain points, which I have highlighted in both the donor and patient examples. These are often called "systemic" issues, and they impact many customers. They must be identified, changed, and remeasured to understand the impact on the customer experience. In the case of the plasma donors, wait time was the systemic issue that needed to be changed. For the patients with the rare disease therapy, it was education around infusion of the medication.

The important point is that pharma CX acts as a critical feedback loop that allows for continuous improvement. Experiences are created with intention, but even the best customer experiences are hard to get right the first time. That's why continuous measurement in real-time is so important.

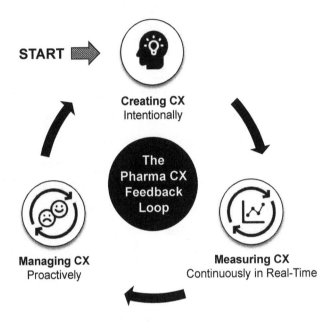

At the end of the day, pharma CX is a *mindset shift* from developing products to intentionally creating, continuously measuring, and proactively managing experiences.

Every important touchpoint. Every time.

CUSTOMER EXPERIENCE IS BOOMING

According to Forrester, customer experience has overtaken price and product as the key brand differentiator. Gartner calls customer experience the "new battlefield," with 80% of companies competing mostly or completely on the basis of customer experience.

CX has become so important that many companies—including Hasbro, MasterCard, and PwC—have added a chief experience officer (CXO) to the executive team.

These CX leaders know that a process for creating, understanding, and managing customer experiences is the launchpad for becoming customer-centric.

Simultaneously, customer experience management (CEM), or "experience management," has become big business and an established practice at most companies. According to a recent study by MarketsandMarkets, the experience management industry is projected to grow from USD 8.5 billion in 2021 to USD 14.9 billion by 2025, at a compound annual growth rate (CAGR) of 11.8%. But the most customer-centric companies do not just collect customer feedback to check a box. That used to happen, for sure, but those days are long gone. Customer feedback is now considered gold. The best companies see it as an asset and use it strategically to retain customers and attract new ones.

Pharma has that same opportunity with pharma CX.

Or does it?

A NOTE ON REGULATORY CONSTRAINTS

Pharma certainly faces regulatory and compliance constraints that other industries do not face. This can limit the extent to which pharma can create and manage customer experiences.

Specifically for HCPs, the federal anti-kickback law prohibits any form of renumeration intended to reward or influence prescribing behavior. Many states have also created a version of this law. Examples of activities that are prohibited include:

- Providing a gift to HCPs to encourage the prescribing of a specific medication
- Awarding research grants to high-prescribing physicians
- Purchasing services from HCPs at exorbitant fees

The Physician Payments Sunshine Act (PPSA) is another federal law that aims to improve transparency regarding payments to HCPs. This law requires pharma manufacturers to disclose to the Centers for Medicare and Medicaid

Services (CMS) any payments or other transfers of value made to physicians.

This notion of a transfer of value has broad implications for pharma CX. For example, pharma can't communicate to HCPs that patient support programs will reduce their workload because that would be something of value, which is not allowed for compliance. However, these programs often make the process of patients accessing the medication easier. It can be a slippery slope.

In addition, Pharmaceutical Research and Manufacturers of America (PhRMA) has created a voluntary code that most pharma companies abide by. The code governs the relationships between industry and HCPs. The PhRMA code puts common sense guardrails on pharma-sponsored meals and entertainment, gifts, continuing medical education, and consulting agreements.

Regarding interactions with patients, there is less clarity.

First of all, in most countries, direct-to-patient pharmaceutical product advertising is not permitted (the United States being the major exception), and where it is permitted, it must be conducted in full compliance with country laws, regulations, and/or relevant codes of practice.

PhRMA has offered "Principles on Interactions with Patient

Organizations." This is to prevent pharma companies from exerting undue influence on the actions of patient organizations. Yet, there is nothing from PhRMA to date on pharma interactions with individual patients.

The International Federation of Pharmaceutical Manufacturers and Associations (IFPMA) provides some guidance on pharma-patient interactions. They note that it is important for pharma to observe clear ethical boundaries when interacting with patients and caregivers, individually or as part of patient organizations. Most of their focus is on ethical guidelines around hiring patients as consultants, advisors, or speakers at internal company meetings.

While the specific laws and guidelines are murky at best, it is clear that since pharma is interacting with patients more and more, these interactions must be carefully monitored to prevent abuse. Thanks to the latest specialty therapies (especially rare disease drugs), a single patient can represent significant revenue to a pharma company. That's a powerful incentive to target potential patients and to be closely involved with their care. The closeness of the relationship needs to be monitored for ethical considerations. For example, Alexion Pharmaceuticals agreed to pay $13 million to resolve allegations that it provided improper financial assistance to patients taking Solaris through a patient assistance program (PAP).

Compliance oversight of patient outreach activities is critical, as are strict firewalls between the patient-facing and marketing activities of the organization. For example, having nurse educators or case managers report directly to sales/marketing is a clear ethical violation.

So, does pharma have the same opportunity with pharma CX as in other industries after considering these regulatory hurdles?

Absolutely!

Effective and memorable customer experiences are not about kickbacks; they are about fostering positive emotional interactions between customer and company. Yes, pharma needs to carefully consider regulatory and compliance guidelines, especially as it relates to HCPs. This is true for everything pharma does. You'll face those same regulatory hurdles when creating ad campaigns, but it would be absurd to suggest that regulations prevent you from creating those campaigns. Pharma has the ability and the responsibility to deliver its customers positive feelings better and more often than any other industry. After all, pharma saves lives and provides better quality of life!

CENTRAL ROLE OF LEADERSHIP

Pharma CX begins and ends with pharma leadership.

Leadership must embrace the idea that customer experience matters, that it's worth spending time and resources on, and that it is the right thing to do for both the patient and the company.

Pharma leaders must make sure the entire organization understands patient-centricity. This is not just the responsibility of the patient-support-services team. Simple acts like regularly sharing patient stories go a long way. These stories have to come from the C-suite on a consistent basis. The entire company needs to understand that the mission is to go the extra mile to support patients!

How many pharma companies have a CXO as part of their executive team? I could not find any. Having one would go a long way toward establishing the importance of customer experience to the organization. Especially in pharma, where so many different teams are siloed with their own specific purpose (such as Medical Affairs, Brand teams, Sales, and Research), a CXO provides alignment across the organization to ensure these teams are primarily focused on the customer. This role could also include a patient-advocacy component, which would align patient experiences with the aptness of the tactics employed to deliver them.

With or without a CXO, pharma leadership faces this question: "As an organization, what can we do *today* to put the patient first and deliver the best possible experience to our patients?"

Leadership must also encourage each employee at a patient-centric pharma organization to ask themselves *this* question, every day: "What can *I* do today to create a better experience for our patients?"

When both pharma leaders and *all* employees are focusing on the patient experience every single day, then patient-centricity becomes real. Yes, all employees. Pharma CX applies to both commercial *and* clinical.

Pharma leaders must embrace pharma CX for it to be a reality! Deliberately create the experiences you want your customers to have, consistently *listen* to patients about the experiences they *are* having, and *proactively manage* those experiences. *Continuously.*

It starts and ends there.

The rest of this book will largely focus on how to do this at the highest level.

NO, CX ISN'T JUST MARKET RESEARCH

Pharma CX has similarities with market research, but pharma manufacturers who understand the differences have a huge advantage.

You might be thinking that pharma CX sounds like market research, and as we all know, pharma does *a lot* of that!

Yes, pharma CX is similar to market research, but there are few distinctions that are important to understand.

Clearly, market research provides great value when it comes to positioning a product for commercial success. From preclinical to post-launch, market research identifies the unmet needs of a target population, confirms market viability, tests concept and potential messaging, determines appropriate pricing, tracks awareness and usage, and more.

Yet, certain principles that are fundamental to market research create limitations around *creating, measuring,* and *managing* the customer experience in pharma.

Before I touch on the differences, there is one important similarity that remains vital to both pharma CX and market research—adverse-event reporting. In market research and in pharma CX, any patient comment that references an adverse event from their current medication must be flagged, reported by CX leaders, and communicated to pharmacovigilance teams. (Secret #20 provides more detail on adverse-event reporting and the importance of choosing a partner who is experienced in this area.)

Now, let's focus on the key differences between pharma CX and market research.

SAMPLE VS. CENSUS

Market researchers usually reach out to a small sample of customers (typically patients or HCPs) for feedback on a wide variety of strategic topics and focus on aggregate results and trends.

Pharma CX reaches out to *all customers* around a specific

touchpoint, sometimes called a "moment of truth," as mentioned in Secret #1. While there are rules to avoid over-surveying an individual customer, pharma CX focuses on measuring specific moments so that pharma companies can manage customer outcomes and perceptions.

POINT-IN-TIME VS. ONGOING

Market researchers are focused on getting an answer to a specific strategic question, which results in studies with a distinct beginning and end. The study is "in the field" for a predetermined period or until certain quotas (e.g., 200 HCP completed surveys) are met.

With pharma CX, there is an *ongoing* dialogue between the customer and pharma that happens in real-time. These conversations never end because there are always new insights to uncover to improve the customer experience at key touchpoints. The ongoing nature of pharma CX also allows the proactive *optimization* of experiences based on the continuous measurement of them. For example, we know that the initial information provided to patients in a clinical trial is key to their overall experience and their likelihood to continue in the trial. By measuring this touch-point consistently for each new patient who joins the trial, the pharma manufacturer can adjust the materials for future trials and then determine whether those adjustments had the expected impact on the patient experience.

AGGREGATE VS. INDIVIDUAL

Market researchers may ask about a new logo, a new message, or how our drug stacks up to the competition but cannot share specific feedback from any individual respondent because market researchers operate under an oath of respondent anonymity. In turn, market research is focused on reporting findings in the aggregate often through graphs, tables, and charts. For example, the following is a "cross tab" table that is used frequently in market research.

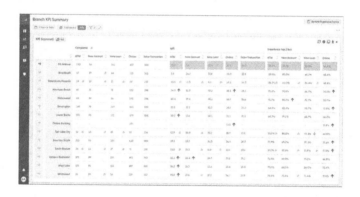

With pharma CX, the patient provides feedback about a recent experience—for instance, an unproductive discussion with a case manager about insurance coverage for a new medication—and pharma can follow up to "close the loop" with that *individual* patient, ask additional questions, and resolve the situation. For example, the following is an alert used in pharma CX to follow up with a customer who had a poor experience.

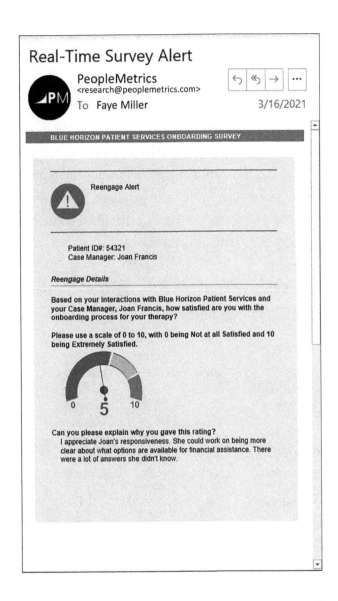

Real-Time Survey Alert

PeopleMetrics
<research@peoplemetrics.com>

To Faye Miller

3/16/2021

BLUE HORIZON PATIENT SERVICES ONBOARDING SURVEY

Reengage Alert

Patient ID#: 54321
Case Manager: Joan Francis

Reengage Details

Based on your interactions with Blue Horizon Patient Services and your Case Manager, Joan Francis, how satisfied are you with the onboarding process for your therapy?

Please use a scale of 0 to 10, with 0 being Not at all Satisfied and 10 being Extremely Satisfied.

0   5   10

Can you please explain why you gave this rating?
I appreciate Joan's responsiveness. She could work on being more clear about what options are available for financial assistance. There were a lot of answers she didn't know.

"Closing the loop" enables the *proactive management* of customer experiences and maintains standards around PII, as the patient always provides permission to be contacted. Secret #17 has more details.

It isn't just about acting on the individual, however. Pharma CX (like market research) also reports findings in the aggregate through charts, graphs, and tables. But instead of delivering these results through a PowerPoint report that takes weeks, or even months, to produce, results are available in real-time in software platforms like PeopleMetrics to any employee who has access.

The following table summarizes the key differences between market research and pharma CX.

	Market Research	Pharma CX
Communication with customer	One-way	Two-way (encouraging dialogue)
Analysis	Aggregate	Individual and aggregate
Audience	Sample	Census
Access to results	Market research team and product sponsor	Everyone
Length of survey	Long	Short/brief
Timeframe	Weeks/months	Real time
Incentives	Usually required	Limited/optional
Timing	Point in time	Continuous
Purpose	Strategic	Strategic and operational
Participant identity	Anonymous	Identified

PHARMA CX DRIVES PATIENT-CENTRICITY

CX leaders know that customer feedback is not effective if hoarded within organizational silos, and that to be truly customer-centric, customer feedback must be shared in real-time with the people who are serving the customer every day.

In this way, experience management has disrupted traditional market research in all industries. In market research, a study is commissioned, it ends, and the firm analyzes the results and delivers a report a month (or more) later. The reality is that those reports rarely find their way to the people serving the customer every day.

How times have changed! Now with experience management (and pharma CX!), customer feedback in most industries is provided in real-time at the most granular levels of the organization. Now companies know their customer satisfaction or Net Promoter Score (NPS) on a minute-to-minute basis, how far away they are from their goal (great CX companies provide departmental and even individual goals), where they are strong, and where they need to improve. There is also a process to follow up and "close the loop" with individual customers who have had poor experiences (e.g., managing the customer experience) and work on larger initiatives to improve CX overall.

CX leaders know that customer experience feedback is

most effective when thoughtfully shared in real-time with the people who can act on it. Can you envision an environment where the voices of pharma customers are shared in real-time with the people tasked with making sure their experience is excellent every day?

I can because I see it every day with my company's pharma clients.

The result is a more consistent and positive experience across the treatment journey in ways that were once not possible.

Pharma CX programs enable HCPs to offer better patient support services (see Secret #8), follow up with patients who do not feel prepared to begin new treatments or medications (see Secret #17), create more effective communications for clinical trials (see Secret #5), develop digital patient engagement technologies that actually engage patients (see Secret #9), and much more.

But most importantly, our pharma CX programs help pharma companies become truly patient-centric.

Their employees are empowered to create better experiences for their customers and have the real-time information to do so at their fingertips. These employees understand what they can do today to create a patient-centric organization.

It's how patient-centricity becomes real.

THE MORAL IMPERATIVE

My company, PeopleMetrics, has had the great fortune of working with companies across different industries for twenty years, helping them intentionally create, continuously measure in real-time, and proactively manage CX. Boutique hotels, exclusive auction houses, large retail banks, private aviation services, large telecommunications companies, high-end restaurants, and more.

Pharma CX feels different. The stakes are higher. It's not just an opportunity to connect with customers on a deeper level. It's a moral imperative for pharma, and companies like PeopleMetrics, to focus on. We must make the experience patients have in clinical trials or onboarding onto a new medication as good as checking into a Four Seasons, creating a playlist on Spotify, or riding a Peloton.

The stakes of a customer experience in pharma can literally be life and death. For example, PeopleMetrics has consistently found that the experience a patient has with patient support services has a direct impact on their preparedness to onboard onto a new medication. And from a financial standpoint, increasing the likelihood that a new patient onboards and adheres over time to a new therapy delivers a direct return on investment (ROI), especially to those in the orphan drug category where annual revenue can be hundreds of thousands of dollars per patient. In addition, there is ample evidence that most pharma product launches have produced disappointing results in recent years. Secret #7 dives into why pharma no longer launches products but experiences and why this provides the best opportunity to maximize the ROI of new product launches.

Delivering a great customer experience these days not only is the right thing to do for the patient, it's good business too.

So, how do the very best companies consistently deliver exceptional customer experiences? One secret is that they map the customer journey and deliberately design experiences that create an emotional connection with the customer. Secret #3 explores customer journey mapping.

SECRET
#3

THE CUSTOMER JOURNEY

**Pharma CX leaders emulate the very best
CX companies by creating experiences
and mapping the customer journey.**

Those great experiences you have at your favorite hotel, coffee shop, restaurant, or website do not happen by accident. These companies are experts at mapping the customer journey and intentionally creating the experiences you love. They leave nothing to chance.

What's often missing in pharma that is omnipresent in these other industries is the unwavering commitment to building the customer journey with intention and creating emotional connections with their customers. Emotionally invested customers are more loyal, recommend more often, and have a higher customer lifetime value (CLV).

Customers will experience your company regardless of whether you prioritize CX. What CX leaders know, and what pharma CX leaders must understand, is that when you *intentionally craft those experiences,* you can create much better outcomes. CX leaders orchestrate the way customers feel after each key touchpoint. From there, the emotional bond with customers grows.

CX leaders also know that *consistency is everything* when it comes to the customer experience. A great experience at a store will be canceled out by a poor experience on a website or a frustrating experience calling into a contact center.

For these reasons, CX leaders are obsessed with mapping the customer's journey, ensuring a consistent experience across all touchpoints and ultimately an emotional connection with the customer. They also understand that the customer journey is a personalized journey, imagining each individual as a complete human, rather than just a consumer. For example, Starbucks famously referred to their stores as a "third place" outside the home and work where people can gather and build a sense of community.

So, what is customer journey mapping? It begins with identifying all the possible touchpoints or interactions you have with your customers. You may be thinking, "We already map our patient journey," but pharma's approach to patient-journey mapping is usually better described as a process flow. It's focused on the end results of medication rather than on understanding the patient's journey and feelings along the way. Let's walk through how this might work in a familiar industry like hospitality to see how a journey map is different. How does a hotel guest interact with a hotel, from the beginning of the experience to the end?

1. **Digital:** A customer lands on the hotel's webpage first—whether that's through a website like booking.com, a TripAdvisor review, or a direct Google search inquiry—where they figure out everything they need to know about the hotel: the location, the cost, and the amenities. The digital experience is the first touchpoint for most hotel customers, and it's an important one. Rather than simply evaluating whether they have a web presence, CX leaders try to understand the experience of visiting those sites. They ask themselves: *Was the information accessible? Is it easy for visitors to use a credit card on the website, and do they feel secure doing so? Did an email confirmation arrive in their inbox soon after they placed the online reservation?*

2. **Contact center:** Many hotel guests have questions about their stay before they arrive at the hotel, so the next touchpoint is likely a contact center, online chat, or even a person answering the phone at the hotel. To evaluate the quality of this interaction, CX leaders would ask: *Was the person on the phone knowledgeable?*

Respectful? Friendly? Was the person able to answer the customer's questions on the first call?

3. **In person:** Once guests actually arrive at the hotel, the touchpoints are almost endless. They may interact with the valet upon arrival and get help with their luggage from a bellhop. They're directed to the front desk to check in and possibly helped in finding the elevator to their room. The customer might call the concierge to ask for dining recommendations or order room service, dine at restaurants within the hotel, visit hotel spas, and exercise in the fitness center. Each of these items is a potential customer touchpoint. Checking out, whether on the room television, on an app, or at the front desk, is another key touchpoint. CX leaders have thought about each of these touchpoints. They're constantly wondering: *Was the check-in process easy and efficient? Did the front desk refer to the customer by their name, and did they pronounce it correctly? Was the room clean and easy to find? Did the hotel deliver what they promised on the website (e.g., free rollaway bed)? Was the checkout process easy?*

4. **Post-visit:** Even after a guest checks out, the touchpoints continue when they retrieve their vehicle. After they get home, they may have questions on the final bill or call the hotel about a lost item. Often, the final post-visit touchpoint is asking the customer for feedback

about their experience. Make sure you include this in your list! *Was the post-stay survey mobile friendly? Did it take a long time to complete? Did the customer get a timely follow-up if they indicated the experience was subpar?*

Now, let's consider how the customer journey applies to pharma with the example of a patient who has been prescribed a new medication and is using a pharma company's patient support services provided by a pharma company to seek help with the onboarding process and with managing their disease.

1. **Digital:** A patient often first turns to digital engagement technologies, including websites, apps, and portals. Enabling easy patient enrollment into a patient support program digitally is critical, both because of COVID-19 and because our lives are largely now digital-first. After enrolling, a patient might also use digital technology to look for information to help them navigate their prescription drug benefits. They may be curious about a PAP that offers copay help or discount coupons. The patient may look for information on available treatment centers and transportation options. The patient's physician might also turn to a website or physician portal that contains guidance on preauthorization help regarding health plan approval to prescribe the new drug. The digital experience is critical for all pharma companies because the web is often the first place customers

turn to for the answers they need. Secret #9 has more information on patient perceptions of pharma's digital engagement offerings, but here are questions to consider as you start to evaluate your digital presence. Ask yourself: *Was it easy to enroll in the patient support program? Was it easy to find the most important information? Was it well organized? Easy to log in? Personalized?*

2. **Contact center:** Next, patients often turn to patient support services or call centers manned by case managers or representatives to get answers to their questions. These contact centers are important hubs of information and support that patients rely on to manage their disease. For patients with rare diseases, case managers are an invaluable resource as they can provide information on financial assistance, PAPs, transportation options, treatment centers, and much more. Patients increasingly count on the people who help them manage their disease being just a phone call away. To ensure these providers are meeting (and exceeding) expectations in these experiences, pharma CX leaders are asking: *Are patient support service phone numbers easily accessible? Is it easy to enroll in a patient support program? Was it easy for the physician to share this information with patients? Are case managers knowledgeable? Empathetic? Available? Treating patients with respect?*

3. **In-person:** For certain medications with complex

administration, nurse educators meet with patients in their homes to answer questions about the disease and the new medication. Educating patients about a complex new drug and teaching them how to take it properly, especially if it's an injectable, is very effective in a face-to-face setting. Nurse educators also visit HCPs to educate them on the disease state and their company's medication. In the world of COVID-19, nurse educators also meet with patients and HCPs "face-to-face" via telehealth. Indeed, information on patient support services are now often delivered from an HCP to a patient via a telehealth session as well. Incorporating an enrollment program directly in a telehealth visit is vital to patient adoption with COVID-19 limiting travel. Telehealth is a digital-meets-in-person touchpoint that will certainly exist well beyond the height of the COVID-19 pandemic. To make the most of this hybrid, and of in-person visits, it's important to ask: *Did the nurse educator arrive on time? Are nurse educators clear in their communication? Was the patient comfortable administering their new medication after meeting with the nurse educator? Did the nurse educator leave behind literature that is easy to understand? Was it easy for the patient to enroll into the patient support program directly in a telehealth visit with their physician?*

4. **Post-Onboarding:** Following up with patients to make sure that they adhere to the prescribed therapy regimen

and care plan is best practice. So much work is done to enable patients to access their new medication, pharma must work just as hard to make sure that patients are getting the health benefits from using and staying on that medication. Check-ins with patients via surveys six months and twelve months after onboarding is an excellent way to maintain a pulse on patient adherence. And surveying all patients, at least once a year, about their overall experience with patient support services and their medication is always a good idea. These relationship surveys are a cornerstone to an effective pharma CX program (see Secret #10). Questions you might ask to make your customer relationships better include: *Has the patient had any issues traveling with their medication? How easy has the medication been to administer? Has the patient been able to reach their case manager to answer questions?*

IDENTIFY "MOMENTS OF TRUTH"

You will identify numerous touchpoints with your pharma customer, but identifying which ones are "moments of truth" is key to creating the best experiences possible. A moment of truth is one where if it goes poorly, a customer outcome is in jeopardy. For example, as a result of a moment of truth, a patient may not onboard or a physician not prescribe.

But how do you determine which touchpoints are "moments of truth"?

It's not as difficult as it sounds. The key question is: how much pain will your customer incur if a touchpoint does not go well?

Prioritize those touchpoints with the biggest potential impact. Great care should be taken to ensure that any moment that might cause irrevocable pain will meet and exceed each customer's expectations. Each moment-of-truth experience must be excellent and ideally should create an emotional connection with the customer!

Let's make creating customer experiences in pharma real with an example. Transportation to treatment centers is often a moment of truth for patients. This has been even more true during the COVID-19 pandemic, as transportation options for patients and caregivers are limited. Consider the following experiences that patient support services could create to help patients with transportation to treatment centers:

1. Have treatment centers listed on a patient support services website (or available with case managers at contact centers).

2. Have treatment centers listed plus public transportation options (including directions from the public transportation drop-off site to treatment center).

3. Use a company like Circulation to offer patients a coupon code for a free or discounted roundtrip ride on Uber or Lyft to the closest treatment center.

Pharma can intentionally create exceptional customer experiences. They must think beyond access, which is undoubtedly important. There are other opportunities to create emotional experiences customers will remember and tell others about. So, which of the three experiences above would create an emotional bond with the patient? There's little doubt it's the third one.

Keep in mind that the experiences you create around customer moments of truth must be continuously measured and proactively managed to ensure patient-centricity. In fact, moments of truth are the first place to employ a continuous listening program with your pharma customer.

Remember, the customer journey for patients should be more than a treatment journey; it's a whole human journey! Pharma has an opportunity to expand its thinking around how to help people—it's not just about medication access; it's about helping people live better lives.

How? Here are a few very simple ideas. You might consider providing:

- Childcare services

- Parking assistance
- Housework assistance including cleaning or handy work
- Meals
- Mental health support
- Access to meditation apps or techniques
- Fitness and nutrition help
- Concierge transportation services

While some of the suggestions above may make your internal regulatory teams nervous, all would help provide a frictionless experience for patients to both obtain their medication and achieve better outcomes. There must be a balance between the "do no harm" mentality of internal regulatory teams and creating customer experiences that patients love. There is so much more pharma can do for its customers!

For example, more than 30% of people with diabetes also have depression. Would better mental health through meditation or access to mental health professionals help these patients have better outcomes? Most definitely.

Plus, it is well established that exercise is a natural way to reduce depression and anxiety. Pharma could partner with fitness organizations like Peloton to offer complimentary indoor exercise classes and content for patients on certain medications. Would that help adherence and result in better medical outcomes? You bet. Is this beyond the scope of pharma's role in the patient experience? Possibly. All I am asking you is to consider expanding what is possible with regard to creating an emotional connection with your customer. My point is that pharma has an incredible opportunity if it changes its mindset on what it means to support patients. Financial access is still very important, especially these days with many out of work. However, there is much more pharma can do to support the full human journey!

YOU CAN DO THIS!

One final word. You can create a customer journey map without spending months on it or hiring expensive consultants. But, if you make the process too complicated or involve too many people within your company, customer journey mapping can take on a life of its own.

A typical customer journey map should be completed in a couple of weeks. Your job is to identify all the customer touchpoints, prioritize which ones are your "moments of truth," deliberately create experiences around these moments (including some of the ones mentioned in the past section on the human journey), and then determine how many of them can be continuously measured in real-time and proactively managed inside your budget. The immediate goal is to get continuous and real-time customer feedback rolling in so that you can begin to understand and proactively manage your customer's experience at moments of truth. Over time, you will see that this impacts customer outcomes and drives business results.

PHARMA CX IN CLINICAL AND COMMERCIAL

SECRET #4

REAL-TIME, AT ALL TIMES

**Pharma companies who embrace
pharma CX extend it to clinical
and commercial experiences.**

To fully embrace pharma CX, you must ensure that the customer experience is pervasive throughout the organization, from clinical to commercial. Patient experience is paramount, and so are the experiences of other stakeholders who impact the patient experience—namely, HCPs and caregivers.

Commercial and clinical. Every moment of truth. Every time.

This may sound daunting. How can we intentionally create, continuously measure, and proactively manage all these experiences? Isn't this expensive? The truth is, it costs a fraction of your market research budget, and the investment is well worth it.

But before we get there, let's first introduce the types of clinical and commercial experiences I am referring to.

CLINICAL PHARMA CX

When I refer to the patient experience for clinical trials, I am *not* referring to the experience with the efficacy of the medication. What I am referring to is everything else the patient experiences, including enrollment process, informed consent materials, key milestones, and more.

Within clinical trials, not only is it possible to create exceptional patient experiences and get continuous patient feedback in real-time—forward-thinking pharma companies are already doing it!

Creating customer experiences and collecting patient feedback in clinical trials is not without its challenges. However, leading pharma companies are overcoming these challenges to improve future protocol design, fine-tune recruitment strategies, drive retention, increase diversity in patient trial participants, and more. The return on investment can be huge. Secrets #5 and #6 take a deep dive into pharma CX in clinical trials.

Worthy of note, the FDA's Patient-Focused Drug Development (PFDD) initiative aims to include patient feedback *throughout the clinical trial.* The best pharma companies are embracing this guidance and proactively getting feedback from patients throughout clinical trials.

Let's go through a basic example of how pharma CX applies to clinical trials. The diagram below shows a real-time patient (or caregiver) feedback loop in a clinical trial setting. A survey is triggered based on a specific patient touchpoint or "moment of truth," such as receiving clinical trial literature, transportation to trial site, or a patient beginning a trial (usually within one month of starting). Measurement of patient experiences in these moments is often done through anonymous surveys provided at the trial site (for more on specific questions to ask, see Secret #6)—usually via a generic link on a patient handout or an iPad (for more on generic link surveys, see Secret #18).

Once a patient or caregiver submits a survey, their feedback is available in real-time for the pharma company to understand and act on to improve the patient experience in future trials. Please note that since clinical trial surveys are anonymous, there is not an opportunity to proactively manage individual customer experiences or "close the loop" on any specific patient issues. However, management of the patient experience in clinical trials is still possible by gathering continuous feedback and using these insights to make changes to the protocol for future clinical trials. Once the protocol has been changed, the patient or caregiver experience can be remeasured to assess the impact of the change. Here is the pharma CX feedback loop in action for clinical trials (see Secret #1).

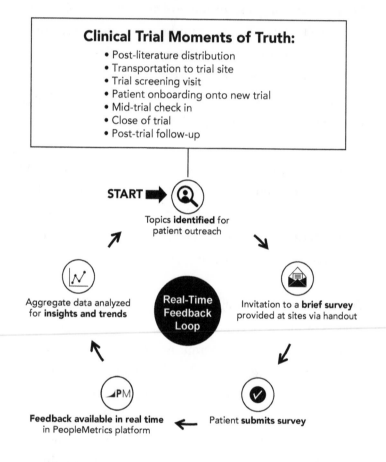

Clinical Trial Moments of Truth:
- Post-literature distribution
- Transportation to trial site
- Trial screening visit
- Patient onboarding onto new trial
- Mid-trial check in
- Close of trial
- Post-trial follow-up

START ➡

Topics **identified** for patient outreach

Aggregate data analyzed for **insights and trends**

Real-Time Feedback Loop

Invitation to a **brief survey** provided at sites via handout

Feedback available in real time in PeopleMetrics platform

Patient **submits survey**

Let's look at this cycle in action.

A few years ago, a global pharma company fielding clinical trials in oncology was looking to adopt a more patient-centric approach to the materials shared with patients as they joined the trial.

There was a belief within the company that the complex language and design of the materials originally created were discouraging patients from reading, understanding, and remembering important study details. The company wanted to create an easier and better experience for the patients in the trial. PeopleMetrics instituted an ongoing pharma CX program to help the company continuously capture feedback from patients after receiving the materials.

The survey was administered in eight countries and six languages. At clinical trial sites, patients were provided a survey link which let them choose whether to complete the survey anonymously, either onsite or at home. The survey was designed to quantify patient feedback on awareness of materials, perceptions of language used, and efficacy of the materials' visual layout.

Most patients were aware of the materials and, after reading them, felt knowledgeable about the topics. However, results *showed that 50% of patients still had questions after reading the materials and 30% said the visual display of information needed improvement.*

Based on patient feedback, the company redesigned the materials to be more visually appealing and include more relevant information. The newly designed customer experience made a big difference! These materials were immediately deployed for use in a separate oncology clinical trial protocol, and the patient experience has since improved.

This is an example of the iterative nature of pharma CX. This company was not sure their trial literature was going to result in an exceptional customer experience. So, they intentionally created an experience around the literature, measured it, and adjusted the experience based on patient feedback, all to the benefit of patients in future protocols.

COMMERCIAL PHARMA CX

On the commercial side, as more providers offer patient support services, creating customer experiences and getting real-time feedback as they interact with these services is paramount. Managing those experiences is even more important.

Touchpoints for patient support services are similar to those in CX (see Secret #3)—digital patient engagement technologies (websites, patient portals, apps), contact centers (case managers), in-person (nurse educators, telehealth), and post-onboarding (six-month, twelve-month check-ins). And as in CX, consistency of the experience is the name of the game in patient support services. For example, a great experience with a case manager can be canceled out by a poor experience with a digital patient portal.

Patient support services are the heart of commercial pharma CX and are often a key part of product launches (see Secret #7). It's so important that there is an entire section of this book dedicated to patient support services (Secrets #8–17). It's important to note that pharma CX applies to all medications, even those that are less complex and do not offer high-touch patient support services. In Secret #11, I introduce a Patient Hierarchy of Needs model that applies to any medication. Patient needs such as financial security, medication administration, and a support system apply to all therapies. The process of fulfilling these needs will differ greatly depending on the complexity of medication. Rare disease drugs often come with an in-house patient support services team with case managers, while mass-market medications teams offer digital support to fulfill almost all patient support needs. However, while pharma CX tactics may differ depending on the complexity of the therapy, it is always necessary to create experiences that fulfill patient needs and foster emotional bonds.

The diagram below describes how pharma CX works in patient support services. Here, a patient or HCP has an experience—usually around a moment of truth such as a welcome call, first infusion, change in insurance, or attending an event (remember, these experiences should be intentionally created by the pharma company, not happening by chance).

Then, an email or SMS survey is sent to the respondent, they submit their feedback, and their responses are available in real-time through a software platform like PeopleMetrics. If the respondent had an issue, it is flagged, and an alert is sent out to a person at the company who can follow up, proactively manage the experience, and "close the loop" (see Secret #17). Results are aggregated and available in real-time to identify systemic issues around the customer experience.

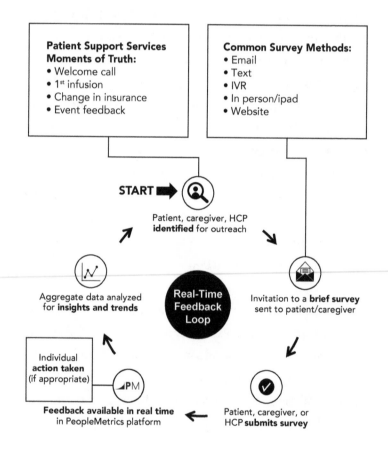

Here's an example we saw unfold in real-time at PeopleMetrics.

A global pharmaceutical company wanted to create a high-touch experience for their patients and chose an assigned-case-manager model for their patient support services offering in the rare disease space. A key benefit of this high-touch model is the ability to provide a support experience catered to individual patient needs. The company identified patient perceptions of their case manager interactions as a "moment of truth."

PeopleMetrics instituted a pharma CX program to help the company capture the experience of patients on an ongoing basis. Immediately after patients interacted with case managers, they were emailed survey invitations. Alert notifications were triggered for any negative feedback so responsible parties would be notified in real-time of any patients who had unresolved issues (see Secret #17).

What did we find?

First, high case manager satisfaction scores showed that the case manager model provided a strong base to serve patient needs. However, open-ended feedback showed that patients faced distinct barriers in certain conversations with their case managers. Specifically, patients were frustrated when their case manager could not provide answers to questions about their disease state, which is illegal for case managers to discuss.

Patients felt they were not only blocked from having this discussion with their case manager, but that they also weren't given direction as to where to find the answers to their disease state questions. Armed with this information, the company created a completely different experience for these patients. They focused on how to connect patients to the best information about their disease state, including standardizing the process of answering questions that are out of scope for case managers. Other changes to the experience included developing a script for case managers to follow when asked to provide disease state information.

From continuous feedback on the patient experience, our client understood the importance of setting expectations with patients early in the relationship about what types of questions case managers can and cannot answer. This allowed them to create better experiences for patients who had questions about their disease state. Case managers added value by providing patients other convenient avenues for finding disease state information. They began to redirect patients to additional resources over the phone and provided information on their website and other channels.

A case manager training program was instituted to implement these changes over time, and the result was a seventeen-point increase in case manager satisfaction!

SECRET #5

EVEN IN CLINICAL TRIALS

Pharma CX is a game changer for clinical trials...and the FDA is watching!

Even after reading Secret #4, you may still ask yourself—does pharma CX really apply to clinical trials?

The answer is a resounding "yes!"

Pharma CX is key to driving patient recruitment, improving retention, increasing adherence, and reducing patient burden in clinical trials. Moreover, if there are multiple trial sites, delivering a patient experience that is consistent across all of them is a pillar of CX (see Secret #3).

Even more, recent events have made pharma CX in clinical trials even more relevant. Fueled by COVID-19 and the social justice movement, many pharma companies are focusing on diversity in clinical trial recruitment. For example, according to a recent FDA report, African Americans make up about 13% of the US population but less than 3% of participants in oncology or cardiovascular disease studies.

The pharma industry is committed to changing the way clinical trials are organized and in turn the experience of all patients in these trials. For example, Bristol Myers Squibb (BMS) recently committed $300 million in funding to efforts to increase diversity in their clinical trial recruiting. BMS is using these funds to raise disease awareness and education, increase healthcare access, and improve health outcomes for medically underserved populations. They are also building trial sites in underserved communities both urban and rural and training a racially and ethnically diverse group of 250 investigators.

While it is commendable that pharma is seeking to create more inclusive clinical trial populations, they must do more. These underrepresented groups need to have a great experience in the clinical trial after being recruited. It would not be surprising to find that the expectations, needs, and experiences of a disadvantaged population aren't necessarily the same as those of other patients. Pharma can adjust the experience they deliver based on the feedback of these underserved populations, increasing the likelihood that these patients are retained throughout the trial. The good news is that pharma companies have begun to systematically create patient experiences in clinical trials. Clinical teams are evolving from "What we subjected patients to" and "What we occasionally got patient input on" to "What we co-created with patients" and "How the patient's voice is vital to better clinical trial outcomes."

The evolution is expanding beyond pharma companies as well. The FDA's PFDD is a systematic approach to help ensure that patient experiences are incorporated into drug development and evaluation.

A key part of this is obtaining patient feedback to facilitate enrollment and retention and minimize the burden of participation in clinical trials.

What can pharma do to take the lead in including the patient's voice in clinical trials?

First, ensure the *research nurse* at the trial site is the face of patient experience. The feedback they give should be part of your pharma CX program. There are a lot of entities involved in a clinical trial—study sponsor, contact research organization (CRO), country manager, site manager, investigator, study coordinator, etc. But the research nurse (coordinator) is often the point person for a patient—this person serves as the face of the trial, represents the sponsor, and translates the patient experience that the protocol is designed to create.

To drive patient retention and improve patient experience, pharma should focus on educating research nurses about how to deliver an excellent patient experience. Plus, recruiting a diverse range of research nurses will go a long way to enable pharma to understand and deliver a better experience to underserved populations. In turn, including research nurse feedback as part of a comprehensive pharma CX program in clinical trials is best practice. Managing that feedback by making suggestions on how the research nurse could better serve patients is also key.

It's important to remember that caregivers' feedback matters too! Patients don't suffer diseases alone. Caregivers are often the unsung heroes in a patient's clinical trial journey—they are the shuttle to and from the site of care, and they are the ones who support the patient during enrollment; they encourage patients to continue and sit with patients during treatment.

As such, they can be a proxy for patient feedback or provide their own perspective on the clinical trial. A large global pharma client of ours weighed this decision recently in relation to a global clinical trial they were launching. They decided that because feedback was required to improve the trial protocol, then patients were the focus. However, beyond that, caregivers were also included, and all feedback was considered to improve the experience of all trial stakeholders.

Keep in mind that caregivers are an important part of the retention equation—their feedback should be a key part of a comprehensive pharma CX program.

Finally, remember that pharma CX clinical measurements need to be patient-friendly. After making the decision to collect feedback from research nurses, caregivers, and patients, it is important to consider how and when this feedback should be collected. Surveys are effective, but only if they are respondent-friendly. For example, a client of ours had patients in a clinical trial who were sight impaired and required the font size of the survey to be increased. Little things like this are big things to patients. In Secret #6, I will go through specific questions to ask patients and caregivers in a clinical trial.

TRACKING SUCCESS

Often, study sponsors ask us, "What is the value of collecting patient feedback in real-time throughout the trial if we can't really act on the feedback? Once the protocol is set, it is very hard to change."

Asking a patient or caregiver for feedback throughout the trial is a way for pharma to understand whether the experiences they created are working. It is pharma CX in action. Yes, some feedback might not be immediately actionable, but feedback on some matters *is*: satisfaction with trial site, perceptions of trial visit, feeling respected through the process, and more. And over time, patient experience feedback can be linked to metrics like trial retention. Plus, learnings from the patient experience in one clinical trial can be used to inform protocols for future trials.

Measuring the patient and caregiver experience in clinical trials is fast becoming best practice. Knowing site performance on controllable attributes and taking corrective action might make all the difference to patient experience and retention, in this trial or a future one.

Next, let's focus on what questions to ask in your clinical trial pharma CX program.

ASK THE RIGHT QUESTIONS

To get a jumpstart on pharma CX in Clinical Trials, begin with TransCelerate's Study Participant Feedback Questionnaire (SPFQ).

By now, you understand the three critical steps to implementing pharma CX, but you may want to know practically, how do you implement a pharma CX program in clinical trials? What experiences do we need to create? What questions do we ask? How often do we ask them? How do we proactively manage customer feedback?

The good news is TransCelerate has a starting point that will get you most of the way there, at least with patients and caregivers.

TransCelerate is a non-profit organization with a mission to collaborate across the global pharma R&D community to identify, prioritize, design, and facilitate implementation of solutions that can drive the efficient and effective delivery of new medicines.

They have created the Study Participant Feedback Questionnaire (SPFQ) based on a collaboration across a group of pharma companies.

According to TransCelerate, the SPFQ is provided to participants and/or caregivers when appropriate at the beginning, middle, and end of a clinical study. It's intended to improve the patient experience in current and future clinical studies. This questionnaire also provides an indication as to which are the most important experiences to create with intention.

There are three phases of the SPFQ.

PHASE ONE

Phase One is given to study participants within a month of enrollment. There are four mandatory questions, all answered on a 5-point agreement scale (0 = Strongly Disagree, 1 = Disagree, 2 = Neither Agree nor Disagree, 3 = Agree, and 4 = Strongly Agree).

1. I understand the treatment process in this trial (e.g., when and how to take or use treatment).

2. The information given to me before I joined the trial was everything I wanted to know (e.g., visits and procedures, time commitment, who to contact with questions).

3. The information given to me before I joined the trial was easy for me to understand (e.g., visits and procedures, time commitment, who to contact with questions).

4. I felt comfortable asking any questions before I joined the trial.

In Phase One, two optional questions are included if the patient is compensated or technology is required as part of the trial.

5. I understand that I will be compensated, the type of compensation (e.g., cash, gift cards, parking reimbursement), how much, and when.

6. I was adequately informed on how to use the [insert technology being used] in this trial.

These are excellent questions that get at the heart of the experience that pharma needs to create for a new patient in a clinical trial. At this stage, all patients and caregivers must feel fully informed. It's paramount that pharma creates an experience that makes their customers feel this way. These questions hit on the moments of truth around being informed—specifically, the quality of the communication and information provided to the patient or caregiver. As we saw in Secret #4, pharma can create an exceptional experience around clear and well-designed study materials in clinical trials.

Questions around compensation and technology are also important if they are part of your study. PeopleMetrics will often add questions about the patient or caregiver's experience with technology at this point. Overall satisfaction with the technology to date, the technology's ease of use, and the value received are possible additions here.

One other addition in Phase One is a question about general satisfaction with the trial site so far. It is important to understand the participant's overall experience to date, even if it has only been a few weeks. This also gives you a baseline to compare to the experience in subsequent phases.

PHASE TWO

Phase Two is given to study participants during the trial, ideally around the mid-point of the study. There are six questions on the same agreement scale as in Phase One, and the focus of these questions shifts to how well the trial is being executed:

1. Overall, I am satisfied with the trial site (e.g., comfort and privacy of the treatment area, waiting area, parking, ease of access to site, etc.).

2. My trial visits have been well organized.

3. My trial visits are scheduled at a convenient time for me.

4. The staff treats me with respect.

5. I feel comfortable asking questions during the trial.

6. I am satisfied with the answers I have received to my questions during the trial.

Next there are two required yes/no questions:

7. The time taken to collect data is acceptable to me (e.g., in-person visits, questionnaires, forms).

8. The impact the trial has on my daily activities is acceptable (e.g., household chores, work commitments, eating).

And one yes/no question that is optional to include based on whether trial data is being collected directly from the patient.

9. The way in which trial data is being collected is acceptable to me (e.g., in person, online questionnaire, diary, wearable sensors, monitoring machines, technology).

The last three questions in Phase Two are also answered on the agreement scale used previously and are optional based on whether there are medical tests done as part of the trial or technology being used.

10. I am being kept informed of the results of my medical tests done during trial, including during screening (e.g., blood tests, scans, etc.).

11. I am satisfied with [insert technology being used] as part of this trial.

12. I find the [insert technology being used] easy to use.

These questions are a great starting point for the mid-trial touchpoint in the evaluation of the customer experience. Overall satisfaction measures the patient or caregiver's overall evaluation of the experience. And if you ask the same questions in Phases One and Two, you can compare satisfaction results across phases.

The other mandatory questions are excellent for understanding the amount of friction patients and caregivers encounter in the clinical trial experience. When visits are well organized and convenient, it is easier for the patient and makes for a better overall experience. Create experiences like that!

Whether in a clinical trial, buying an automobile, or boarding an airplane, being treated with respect and being able to ask questions (and get answers) are hallmarks of a great customer experience. The final mandatory questions are about the experience the patient or caregiver has around the information they are provided (including the SPFQ!) and the impact of the trial on the life of the patient.

Please note that the optional questions surrounding technology get more detailed in Phase Two. Satisfaction with technology and technology ease of use is found here (remember, you can include these in Phase One as well so you can track changes). Including a question around the value the patient is receiving from the technology as in Phase One is useful here as well. And if there are medical tests being done as part of the trial, include the corresponding question.

PHASE THREE

Finally, Phase Three is given to study participants at their final trial visit. It's meant to gauge the patient experience at the end of the trial.

It begins with two yes/no questions:

1. I was informed when I had completed the trial.

2. I was informed of any future opportunities to access the overall trial results.

The next two questions are on the 0–4 agreement scale noted above:

3. Overall, I was satisfied with the information I received about support after the trial (e.g., future treatment, follow-up contact details).

4. Overall, I was satisfied with my trial experience.

The final question focuses on patient burden in the trial. This question is asked on an expectations scale (0 = Much Less than Expected, 1 = Somewhat Less than Expected, 2 = Same as Expected, 3 = Somewhat More than Expected, and 4 = Much More than Expected).

5. Compared to when the trial started, the overall commitment required was similar to what I expected.

In Phase Three, questions focus on the experience at the end of the trial, including whether the patient was informed the trial was complete and could access the results of the trial. First, there is a measure of the overall experience of the trial. Getting information about future support is important for the patient. And the last question around the patient burden that was promised versus the reality is a great one. It can inform trial literature and improve expectation setting in future trials. These are all experiences pharma can and should create with intention!

We often recommend repeating the technology questions, if appropriate, in the last phase. Understanding the effectiveness of the technology, its ease of use, and utility is key to improving future trial experiences. Don't forget to create the very best technology experience you can for patients.

GETTING PATIENTS AND CAREGIVERS TO PROVIDE FEEDBACK

Obtaining clinical trial feedback is not without its challenges. Small patient populations are often the most significant barrier to overcome. Every experience counts, especially when clinical trial patient populations can be as small as twenty or so in Phase One for certain rare diseases. The key is to make it as easy as possible for patients and caregivers to provide feedback, no matter how small the patient population. This means being flexible with how you collect feedback—the survey should be accessible on the trial site via an iPad or a QR code. The patient also should be able to take the survey from their home (see Secret #18 for details on various modes of data collection).

Also, make it easy for your trial sites to distribute your surveys. All that your trial sites should have to do is provide a handout, QR code, or iPad. Make sure you clearly communicate expectations to site managers and outline the survey's purpose so they understand the importance of this new process. In fact, this should be part of the trial protocol whenever possible.

One tip is to monitor the completion rate of surveys across your different trial sites. This allows you to make sure you're getting adequate participation at each site and follow up with individual site managers if any adjustments need to be made.

Often the best clinical trial candidates for pharma CX are global studies with multiple sites and languages. Here, you can get a good bang for your buck as the overall patient population is larger, the survey the same for each trial site (save for translation into appropriate languages), and the overall response large enough to draw conclusions, make comparisons across sites, and make changes to future trials.

With regard to pharma's increasing emphasis on more diverse patient populations in clinical trials, it is important to closely examine the feedback you get from these patient populations. Compare the answers you receive on the SPFQ across your patient populations to make sure you are meeting the distinct needs of all your patients and providing them with the best experience possible. Remember, recruiting more diverse groups of patients is just the beginning; you must also create an experience that will encourage them to finish the trial.

CREATE THE PERFECT PRODUCT LAUNCH

Pharma CX makes or breaks a product launch, so be sure to prioritize it before your next big launch.

The very best pharma companies no longer launch products; they launch experiences. Clinical efficacy, safety, superiority to alternatives, and ease of use are no longer enough. Customers need more from your pharma company.

A recent McKinsey research study shows that customer experience matters in pharma, even with great medications. The study was conducted among 600 immunologists in Europe and the United States and indicates that when prescribers are fully satisfied with their journey for a particular therapy and with the pharma company's contribution to it, they are *more than twice as likely* to prescribe it as dissatisfied prescribers. By paying more attention to the customer experience (in this case the HCP), companies can not only increase satisfaction but also boost sales and market share.

WHY PHARMA CX MUST BE PART OF LAUNCH PLANNING

The Tufts Center for the Study of Drug Development estimates the cost to bring a single drug to market as $2.6 billion. This includes R&D costs and opportunity costs (but not post-approval R&D, which can drive real costs across the product life cycle closer to $3 billion).

After the drug is approved, the pressure for the commercial side of the business to recoup the R&D investment becomes tangible. And according to a recent McKinsey article, world-class customer experiences can make the biggest impact on a product launch in the first six months post-approval. The performance of a drug in its first six months on the market tends to determine its ultimate market share.

By focusing on intentionally creating an exceptional customer experience using customer journey mapping and moments of truth (as reviewed in Secret #3), pharma can create more successful product launches. This also includes continuously listening to customers in real-time, identifying and resolving points of friction, and "closing the loop" with individual patients and HCPs. By following the pharma CX model, pharma companies can improve key performance indicators such as customer satisfaction and treatment preparedness, improve adherence to therapies, and positively impact their bottom line.

APPLYING PHARMA CX TO PRODUCT LAUNCH

Pharma CX at product launch cannot be accomplished with a few focus groups with patients and HCPs while the drug is in late-stage development.

Instead, you must consider touchpoints and "moments of truth" for both patients and HCPs.

What do *patients* need to maximize positive health outcomes? Are they getting the financial and access support they need to feel confident in therapy? What about emotional support? Do they understand your educational materials? Is the onboarding and welcome process overwhelming patients with too much information? Is it not giving them *enough* information? How does your patient support services program compare to companies with competitive therapy? Are friction points creating risks of non-adherence?

What do HCPs need to effectively support their patients?

Through which channels do they prefer to receive information? How do they prefer to be spoken to? Are the interactions happening today effective? Are they consistently experiencing a problem? If so, what is it and how do we fix it?

Use the answers to these questions to map out the full customer journey (Secret #3), choosing which experiences you want to create. It's also important in these early stages to determine how you plan to measure the effectiveness of each touchpoint, including how often and with what technology. Without a vision for how to measure what you've created in real-time, you won't be able to adequately adapt to the feedback from your customers. With a plan in place before launch, companies can make pharma CX a competitive differentiator that goes beyond clinical efficacy, safety, ease of use, and superiority.

PHARMA CX SECRETS FOR PATIENT SUPPORT SERVICES

THE BEST INVESTMENT YOU CAN MAKE

As demand for patient support services skyrockets, savvy pharma companies are investing more in this area on the front lines of pharma CX.

In "Why Pharma Companies Can't Ignore Patient Services," Accenture points out that 76% of patients expect their pharmaceutical provider to offer patient support services.

And according to another Accenture report titled "The Patient Is IN: Pharma's Growing Opportunity in Patient Services," 85% of pharma companies are expected to dramatically raise their investment in patient support services in the upcoming years.

In a PeopleMetrics study on patient support services among rheumatoid arthritis (RA) patients, we found strong momentum for patient support services, including:

- 52% of RA patients being aware that patient support services were available
- Awareness of over 60% for patient support services offered by leading RA medications Orencia (63%), Enbrel (62%), and Actemera (62%)

As more pharma companies provide patient support services, these services will be the price of admission for all products. For example, a 2020 study by Human Care Systems with pharma executives found that *93% of pharma executives agree that customer experience with patient support services is a top priority for pharma* (emphasis added).

It's clear that patient support services are on everyone's mind, but to further increase awareness for these services, pharma needs to promote them as if they were brands within the company and communicate about them through the same channels they're already using to address the patient.

HCPs have become a primary target for awareness programs around patient support as they usually inform patients that these services are available. Efficacy is always going to trump support services for HCPs, but these services can make the HCP feel better about prescribing the medication.

Yet, for some of our clients, awareness of patient support services is still a big challenge. It comes down to obtaining a budget and specifically allocating dollars to promote awareness of available patient support services. Some patient-support-services leaders express frustration about getting these services on the radar of the sales team members who visit HCPs. For example, it can be hard to know how much time a sales rep spends talking about patient support programs when they visit an office. Plus, staff are often overwhelmed at HCP offices, and there is often a lot of attrition. The bottom line is that understanding how much the patient support services message is being conveyed at HCP offices continues to be a challenge for many.

Given all of this, it's important to take a step back and understand what is important to consider when designing a patient support services program in the first place.

INSOURCED, OUTSOURCED, OR BOTH?

Pharma companies are experts in their therapeutic area, but that doesn't automatically translate into providing world-class support services for those medicines.

Deciding whether you want to insource or outsource your

patient support services team is an important decision, with pros and cons on each side. No matter which option you choose, taking the time to think about what experiences you want your customers to have with support services is key. The creation phase applies to both insourced and outsourced options.

Insourced teams allow for full control over the customer experience. It's easier for internal teams to build internal expertise for complex disease states, and you directly control the patient experience that you are creating. For example, if you want to create an intimate experience for your patients, providing access to assigned case managers is an excellent option.

Patients often experience an emotional bond with their case managers, who are often part of insourced teams. In fact, we find a strong correlation with overall program satisfaction and case manager satisfaction in pharma clients who specialize in rare disease medications. Most of the time, patients have a better experience when a case manager actually cares about them and their journey managing a chronic disease. However, controlling the patient experience comes at a cost. You will likely have to build your own call center operations with case managers, and scaling that as patients onboard can be challenging.

Outsourced teams trade control over the customer experience for scaling and operational expertise. Hubs are experts in providing call center operations, platforms for managing patient access and scaling. However, keep in mind that you still own the patient experience even when the Hub is providing the support services. *And you still must intentionally create the experiences the Hub is going to deliver.* Plus, patients are not cases; they are people. You risk losing that personal touch with your patients when you outsource to a Hub. It may be worth it for certain therapies, but others require the personal touch. In any event, a strong partnership with your Hub is key, so you have input into how the Hub interacts with your patients, complete transparency into the experiences your patients have with the Hub, and the ability to proactively manage these experiences.

The good news is that you don't have to pick one or the other. A hybrid model can strike a balance between controlling the experience and getting the benefits of scale.

WHERE TO BEGIN PHARMA CX IN PATIENT SUPPORT SERVICES

The pharma space is unique in that patients interact with a network of providers to get care (doctors, pharmacies, insurers, etc.), and many of these interactions are outside of your control.

Start with moments of truth within patient support services

that you own—such as patient onboarding or first infusion. Refining and improving these key experiences will provide quick wins early on that can be shared internally and act as a first step in building pharma CX within your company.

The next secret focuses on how digital offerings are key to driving patient satisfaction with patient support services.

GO DIGITAL

Patient adoption of digital engagement offerings will drive a better experience with patient support services.

A key consideration for patient support services teams is creating digital experiences. A recent Accenture study found that 95% of pharma companies are planning to invest in digital patient engagement technologies over the next eighteen months.

And for good reason.

For mass-market medications, your digital offering is likely the full extent of patient support services offered. Even for a rare disease therapy with a small patient population and dedicated case managers, a digital offering is expected and can improve the overall patient experience.

When building out your digital strategy, it's important to understand what your patients need from a digital offering before making your investment. For example, a pharma client of ours invested heavily in a symptom tracker for their patient portal, but when we surveyed patients to ask about their experience, we found that 89% of their patients did not use it. From patient feedback, we found that they did not use this new tool because they already tended to use other symptom trackers available in the market. Our client had built a tool without first tailoring it to the patient's needs. This is an example of creating a customer experience in a vacuum. Asking patients about their experience with other symptom trackers would have saved the company significant time and resources.

In another recent study, PeopleMetrics spoke with over 400 patients to get their perceptions of the patient support services they use, including usage and experience with digital engagement technologies.

This study provided three key insights to consider when building or modifying your digital engagement offering.

1. **Patients primarily use digital engagement offerings to learn more about the support services you provide.**

   We found that the key differentiator for patients who used a digital engagement technology, such as a website or portal, for patient support services is that they had a greater awareness of *all the support services* available

And awareness of specific patient support services was as much as *20% higher* for patients who used a digital engagement offering compared to those who did not.

Building awareness of patient support services has a major impact. We found that most patients are satisfied with a support service once they are made aware of it, and as a result, greater awareness tends to drive higher satisfaction.

Overall satisfaction with patient support services is fifty points higher for patients who used these digital offerings than for patients who did not!

The real challenge for pharma is building experiences around digital engagement technology that are useful to the patient. Remember, pharma CX begins with creating experiences with intention.

2. **Digital offerings are especially effective in helping patients obtain additional resources.**

One of the biggest unmet patient needs is the need for more information on their condition and treatment. This can be a tricky one since patient support services are prohibited by law from providing certain types of information regarding treatment.

However, patients are still looking for a trusted resource to provide this information. By using your digital engagement offering to link patients to third-party organizations and resources, you can instill trust in the patient.

For example, we found that 91% of patients who used a digital engagement offering were satisfied with how their support provider connected them to third-party patient organizations that provided information on their condition.

However, only 71% of patients who did *not* use a digital engagement offering were satisfied with this connection to patient organizations. Again, getting your patients to use your digital offering makes a big difference!

A moment of truth for many patients is obtaining detailed information on their condition. While pharma has some hurdles in fulfilling this experience themselves, the experience still needs to be intentionally created, continuously measured, and proactively managed. Armed with the information above, pharma can still create a positive experience for patients seeking this information by making it easy to find third parties via their digital engagement technologies (and case managers if appropriate).

3. **There is room to improve digital engagement offerings for prior authorization and insurance verification.**

Generally, patients who use digital engagement offerings show higher awareness and satisfaction with their patient support services provider, but there are two instances where using a digital channel has *no impact* on patient satisfaction: prior authorization and insurance verification.

These two often complex tasks are best handled through higher-touch experiences via call center representatives or case managers.

However, keeping this in mind as you create this experience for your patients, you may be able to differentiate your patient services offering by making this experience easy for patients, either digitally or via contact centers. For example, providing notifications and status updates in the digital engagement technology for prior authorization and insurance verification could help guide patients through lengthy approval processes without the need for a phone call with a representative.

The point is that while digital is no doubt important,

creating experiences with intention is more important. What is the best vehicle to deliver the experience your customers need with as little friction as possible? Sometimes the answer is digital, sometimes not.

LOOKING AHEAD

Patients use digital engagement offerings to obtain comprehensive information at their own pace and at scale. Patients want to easily find information on the support services you provide, as well as information on third-party organizations that can help them.

Digital engagement offerings can help patients do that.

As you continue to build and modify your digital footprint, it is important to first spend time intentionally creating the experience you desire. Make sure the digital channel is appropriate. And certainly collect feedback from patients to understand their experiences.

Including questions around patient usage of your digital engagement offerings and their experience with these technologies is best practice in any pharma CX program in patient support services.

START SMALL

The most effective pharma CX programs for patient support services start tiny, with either a relationship survey or a transactional survey around onboarding.

Patients are also consumers. They have smartphones and smart watches. They shop on Amazon. Listen to Spotify. Stay at W Hotels. Watch Netflix. A patient who is onboarding onto a new medication has also had consumer experiences that influence their expectations.

Apple, Peloton, Hyatt—you name it, your patients have probably experienced it.

As we learned in Secret #3, a hallmark of a superior customer experience is one that is consistent, no matter the channel or touchpoint. All the companies listed above work tirelessly to create and deliver an exceptional customer experience.

This rings true for patient support services as well.

Once a customer journey map has been completed with all patient touchpoints included (see Secret #3), moments of truth identified, and experiences created with intention, it's time to measure in real-time. Patient and HCP feedback is critical if you want to know whether the experience you created resulted in the patient experience you expected.

But be careful—it's tempting to try to measure everything all at once. Don't do that. That's how you get overwhelmed. It's important to start with something that you can handle. Get started with what I call "tiny measurements."

There are two tiny measurements you should consider: a relationship survey with all your customers and a transactional survey that focuses on a single moment of truth.

RELATIONSHIP SURVEY (POINT IN TIME)

A relationship survey is a strategic snapshot of the effectiveness of your patient support services program. This is often a good option to begin with—especially if you have not measured the patient and HCP experience with support services previously.

This approach is simple. You reach out to all your current patients (and ideally HCPs), no matter what stage of the treatment journey they are on, and ask them questions about their experiences to date. You get a broader sense of the patient and HCP experience with patient support services, including the high and low points. You also get a baseline to gauge future progress against.

Please note, you will need a separate relationship survey for your patients and their HCP(s). The patient relationship survey should focus on their overall experience with patient support services offered, including specific touchpoints that they have experienced over the past year.

The HCP relationship survey is also about their overall experience but is more focused on the clarity of the communication and literature provided by your patient support team. You can also ask competitors questions about other patient support services offerings they have experienced to get an indicator of relative performance. Asking about how the sales team introduced the available patient support services is another solid line of inquiry.

Relationship surveys are usually longer than other surveys (up to fifteen minutes) and because of this, may require an honorarium, especially for physicians who are used to being compensated for survey feedback. The benefit of the longer survey is that your respondents can provide deeper and more thoughtful feedback. For example, we have had patients say they want digital wallets with their medical information, available nurses with whom to discuss conditions, travel reimbursement for treatment-related travel, and patient events. Hearing recommendations from patients is invaluable to our clients because it gives them the evidence they need to advocate for program changes internally.

Please note, a relationship survey will result in a large volume of responses quickly, so right away you'll have a lot to work with! Results from these surveys guide your future ongoing transactional survey design, as you use this feedback to decide what specific touchpoints and questions should be prioritized.

Whether or not you start with a relationship survey, it's a good idea to conduct one at least once a year to understand the progress you have made with the overall customer experience and identify any emerging issues. It's also a way to make sure you are touching all your patients and HCPs at least once a year.

TRANSACTIONAL (ONGOING)

A second option is to start with a transactional survey on a key touchpoint or moment of truth.

We have found that the *onboarding* touchpoint is often a

moment of truth and the best place to start a pharma CX program in patient support services. It's a great starting point because this moment is often where patients need the most guidance from your support services. They're navigating a recent diagnosis, prescription, and insurance coverage. So, feedback at this point gives you an overview of how well you're serving their needs.

Be prepared, you will likely find something unexpected in your onboarding feedback. One PeopleMetrics client was concerned that patient welcome calls were too long. The patient onboarding process was split into multiple calls that usually took an hour and a half, and they expected patients to indicate that the calls were too long and contained too much information.

Instead, they found that 96% of patients said that the calls were an appropriate length. Patients commented that summary notes from their discussions would be valuable material for them to review ahead of subsequent calls. Prior to fielding the survey, our client was considering reducing the call length and the amount of information covered during the welcome calls, but patients actually wanted *more* detailed information to supplement their call. This kind of insight is only possible through asking patients directly.

This is another important reminder that even when you create experiences with intention, you may not get them right the first time. You do your best to feel what the patient feels when you are creating the experiences. However, only by measuring the actual experience in real-time do you know whether what you created is optimal.

When you implement a transactional survey, make sure you keep them to five minutes or less. Since they are shorter, they won't require an honorarium, but you should expect the volume to be lower than relationship surveys.

The benefit of the transactional approach is that by reaching out to patients and HCPs at a key delivery milestone, the real-time feedback is timely and actionable. You can then immediately follow up with patient concerns at critical moments and "close the loop" on any outstanding issues (see Secret #17). It's tactical and has a strong ROI.

Transactional surveys also allow you to gather targeted feedback that can be used for individual coaching and recognition of case managers. This is the pharma CX feedback loop in action. First, you create a high-touch experience using case managers. Then, you measure patients' actual experiences. Using that information, you proactively manage the patient experience by improving case manager performance. This is essentially creating a new experience for patients that you then measure again to assess the impact of your efforts.

After getting your transactional program started, you can expand it in any number of ways. You can collect customer feedback on everything from case managers, patient liaisons/certified nurse educators (CNEs), specialty pharmacies, digital offerings (websites, apps), HCPs and office managers, first infusion, and key intervals after onboarding.

But first, start with tiny measurements—either a relationship survey or the onboarding "moment of truth" touchpoint survey. You will be glad you did.

In the next secret, I will introduce a model that identifies the key patient needs that your patient support services must fulfill, including specific questions to ask when onboarding a new patient onto a new medication.

	Relationship	Transactional
Timing	Once a Year	Ongoing
Follow Up	Rarely	Yes
Length	10–15 Minutes	Under 5 Minutes
Honoraria	Sometimes	Never
Competitor Questions	Often	Never
# of Touchpoints Covered	All	Usually one
Volume of Responses	Large	Smaller
Primary Objective	Strategic	Tactical
Org. Access to Results	Limited	Extensive

THE PATIENT HIERARCHY OF NEEDS

Patients have a Hierarchy of Needs when they onboard onto a new medication. Creating experiences that fulfill these needs is pharma CX in action!

The patient experience with patient support services matters. *A lot.*

PeopleMetrics has consistently found that patients who have positive experiences with patient support services are *much more likely* to onboard onto their new medication and adhere over time than those who have poor experiences. More details on this important dynamic in Secret #16. For now, the point is that patient experience drives outcomes—not just financial ones, medical ones too.

So, what experiences must patient support services create during the onboarding process to yield a positive patient experience?

PeopleMetrics has developed a "Patient Hierarchy of Needs" model that helps answer this question.

THE PATIENT HIERARCHY OF NEEDS

Our model is based on thousands of patient surveys regarding experiences with patient support services when *onboarding* onto new medications from a range of pharma manufacturers. We chose onboarding because it is a common moment of truth for patient support services teams and one most of our pharma CX programs focused on. The model is based on Maslow's Hierarchy of Needs:

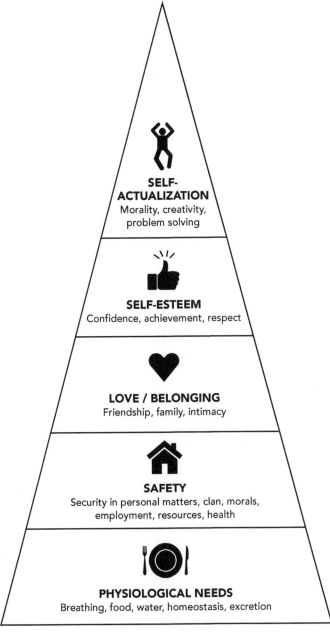

SELF-
ACTUALIZATION
Morality, creativity,
problem solving

SELF-ESTEEM
Confidence, achievement, respect

LOVE / BELONGING
Friendship, family, intimacy

SAFETY
Security in personal matters, clan, morals,
employment, resources, health

PHYSIOLOGICAL NEEDS
Breathing, food, water, homeostasis, excretion

Maslow's Hierarchy of Needs

The Maslow model holds that a person requires certain basic needs to be fulfilled before other higher-order needs are even considered. For example, without physiological needs being fulfilled, such as food, water, and a place to live, most people are not concerned with self-esteem needs such as respect and achievement.

In the diagram below, you can see the Patient Hierarchy of Needs model follows a similar framework:

◢**People**Metrics

Patient Support Services Hierarchy of Needs

GO
Confidence — *"I feel confident that I am prepared for my treatment"*

Support System — *"I can easily get answers to my questions"*

Medication Administration — *"I know how to administer this medicine"*

Logistical Support — *"I know how to get my medication and can get it in a reasonable time frame"*

$
Financial Security — *"I can afford this"*

The model begins with the most fundamental patient need—*financial security*. Patients who can afford the medication move up to the next level. Financial security is oxygen to patients. Without it, they will not onboard onto a new medication. It is here where pharma has rightfully put much of its pharma CX energy with PAPs that help reduce the patient's financial burden and increase access.

The next patient need is *logistical support*. Patients need to know where to get their medicine and be able do so in a timeframe appropriate for their disease state. Knowing where and when they will get their medicine makes patients feel safe. Here is where pharma has an opportunity to do more. Making it easier for patients to obtain their medication helps patients onboard and adhere over time. In Secret #3, there are several examples of how pharma could make it easier for patients to obtain their medication, such as transportation services and childcare.

After that, *medication administration* is paramount. The patient must know how to administer their medication. This is especially important for complex therapies.

The fourth level of needs focuses on the *support system* offered to patients. Patients need to feel like they can easily get their questions answered by a trusted source. Depending on how you deliver the patient support services, this could range from dedicated case managers for rare disease medicines to mobile apps for mass-market products. Patients need to feel that someone is on their side and looking out for them.

The final and highest order patient need is *confidence*. At the end of the day, this is the ultimate patient need that patient support services must fulfill—enabling patients to be confident that they are prepared to begin treatment.

What about self-actualization, Maslow's highest-level need? The best analogy is achieving the outcomes from the medication over time, which is all about adherence. This is a major difference between Maslow's hierarchy and the patient support services hierarchy: while Maslow's hierarchy suggests someone achieves self-actualization last, the patient support services hierarchy suggests that you are *always* attempting to achieve adherence. Indeed, patient support services are responsible for creating, measuring, and managing patient experiences beyond the onboarding phase. Providing support to patients throughout their treatment journey is key to patients achieving the highest order need—good health via adherence.

This model gives patient support services teams a framework to create specific experiences that fulfill each of the five fundamental patient needs when onboarding onto a new medication.

So, which questions do you ask specifically to measure whether these patient needs are fulfilled?

The next five secrets will focus on these questions.

ACCESS IS EVERYTHING

Helping patients feel secure about affording their new medication is priority number one for patient support services.

◢**People**Metrics

Patient Support Services Hierarchy of Needs

In the previous chapter, I introduced a model to help patient support services teams continuously measure in real-time and proactively manage the patient experience during onboarding. For patient support services teams, the first level of patient need that must be fulfilled focuses on access and affordability—*can the patient afford their new medication?* We call this "Financial Security," and it is the fundamental level need in our pyramid.

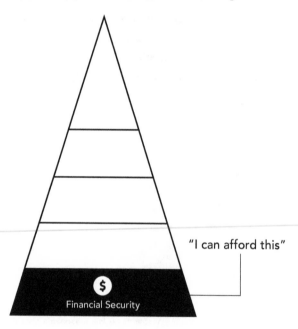

◢**People**Metrics
Patient Support Services Hierarchy of Needs

"I can afford this"

$ Financial Security

Unless the patient can afford their new medication, nothing else really matters. Like Maslow's physiological needs (air, water, food, shelter), a patient is not concerned about higher-order needs unless financial security is fulfilled.

Patient support services teams are keenly focused on creating experiences that help patients with financial access to their medication, and for good reason. Without financial access, nothing else really matters. Financial assistance for patients, support with insurance coverage, and reimbursement and copay assistance are just a few of the ways patient support services help patients fulfill this critical need.

PeopleMetrics's model includes *two questions* that measure the financial security need. Each is asked on a 5-point agreement scale (5 = Strongly Agree, and 1 = Strongly Disagree):

1. *I received the insurance or financial assistance information I needed to begin my treatment.*

2. (Complete if applicable.) *My case manager clearly explained my financial assistance program options (e.g., insurance benefits, copay assistance, etc.).*

The first question can be asked for any type of patient support services program, from a high-touch approach with case managers for rare disease therapies to a digital approach for mass-market medications.

The key is to get an indication as to whether your team

helped the patient get the financial information they need to begin treatment.

Patient support services can have a huge impact here. For example, as one patient noted, "[The patient support] team is friendly and supportive. The first month that I received the drug this insurance year, *the copay plan was very helpful* and enabled me to get the drug, which was great" (emphasis added).

Another patient shared this: "There was a delay with my insurance company *and [my representative] was able to find the financial services* I needed" (emphasis added). These patients clearly feel like they have financial security. Once this is the case, your team can move on to other key issues. And they should. Patient support services must be more than financial assistance! More on that later.

For high-touch patient support services programs with case managers, we also recommend an additional question specific to the case manager's ability to explain financial assistance program options. Ask this if your medication is in the rare disease space and you have case managers helping patients. Patients love case managers, and they help directly with this core financial need. Their impact on the customer experience is profound.

For example, consider this patient's appreciation for their

case manager: "[My case manager] is very friendly and personable. She was a big help in helping me get my first dose of [my medication] when I was *having trouble getting it approved by my insurance*" (emphasis added).

Another patient valued their case managers expertise, saying, "She seems very knowledgeable about the medication and the process for getting it filled and *covered by my insurance plan*" (emphasis added).

Finally, this patient sums up the value that case managers have with regard to financial assistance and keeping the patient on track toward adherence: "They tell me when I can refill before my pharmacy does, so I've been able to build up a bit of a safety net despite only getting one box at a time. The reps also clearly take notes and remember things you mentioned to them from the previous communication. *Also, copay assistance is really a lifesaver*" (emphasis added).

FINANCIAL SECURITY BENCHMARKS

Our Patient Hierarchy of Needs model was developed based on patient feedback from numerous patient support services programs offered by pharma manufacturers or partner Hubs.

One of the benefits of our model is that it includes benchmarks.

Benchmarks are norms that allow you to compare your company to other companies offering patient support services.

In terms of financial security, the goal is that all patients received the insurance or financial assistance required to begin their treatment. Unfortunately, our benchmarks reveal that approximately one out of every four patients feel like this is not happening.

On the other hand, when case managers get involved, *nine out of ten* patients report that their case manager clearly explained their financial assistance program options!

This data describes why the investment in case managers can be worth it, even perhaps beyond small patient populations. Case managers can fulfill the fundamental patient need of financial security. The impact of case managers on the patient experience will be a recurring theme as we move through the model.

What we've found in our client work and independent research is that case managers help in two significant ways. At a base level, they help patients navigate their financial assistance. Whether it's speaking with an insurer, directing patients to support organizations, or explaining coverage, case managers handle much of the burden that would otherwise fall on patients alone.

While we often hear about how helpful case managers are, it's just as common to hear patients talk about the caring demeanor of their case managers. Case managers don't just answer patients' questions, they can also be caring and knowledgeable people to talk to, which can help give patients a sense of financial security.

Case managers are worth every penny in terms of the customer experience for rare disease medications that require this level of support.

LOGISTICAL SUPPORT MATTERS

After patients feel secure about affording a new medication, logistical support should be the primary focus of patient support services teams.

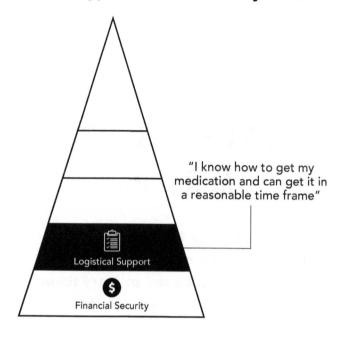

Patient Support Services Hierarchy of Needs

"I know how to get my medication and can get it in a reasonable time frame"

Logistical Support

Financial Security

Even if the patient can afford their new medication, if they do not know how to get it or believe it is too difficult to obtain it, they will not onboard. To understand how patients feel about the logistics of obtaining their medication, PeopleMetrics identified two important questions to ask, each on a 5-point agreement scale (5 = Strongly Agree, and 1 = Strongly Disagree):

1. *[Insert company name] made it easy to find a physical treatment location.*

2. *The time it took to receive the medication after my initial prescription was reasonable.*

The first question focuses on medications that require a physical treatment location, as is common for rare disease drugs. Providing clear communication on where to find a treatment location is critical to new patients, particularly for more complex therapies or those that are delivered through injectables.

In Secret #3, I went through examples of how patient support services teams can imagine different types of patient experiences involving transportation to a treatment facility. Options range from providing the information on a digital engagement technology to providing coupon codes for Uber or Lyft rides through a company like Circulation.

COVID-19 has impacted logistical support in major ways. For example, when shelter-in-place orders made it difficult for patients to find an infusion center, Ocrevus, a multiple sclerosis infusion therapy, leveraged its existing navigator program to help patients find new infusion centers or even schedule home infusions.

Also, in response to COVID-19, BMS partnered with COA/CancerCare, an oncology advocacy group, to deliver free door-to-door patient transportation that made it easy for oncology patients to get to and from their appointments.

Some brands partnered with telehealth providers to help patients get on therapy while avoiding transportation altogether. Many have partnered with third-party telehealth systems to offer patients the option to connect to a care provider via video visits.

The best support teams also continue to help patients easily locate treatment facilities after onboarding. What if a patient is travelling? What if they've moved? What if a pharmacy location closes? Not only do support teams need to assist with all these possibilities, but they also need to make patients aware that these are services they provide. If patients aren't aware of how you can help, then they may not go to the effort of finding a regular treatment location on their own if their situation changes.

Patients notice this help too! One patient shared this: "They seemed to really care, and they went the extra mile *to make sure I knew where to get my medication*" (emphasis added).

HCPs also appreciate the logistical support that patient support services provide. One physician noted that the patient support services team is "always willing to help with *getting my patients on the medication*, getting approved, and with compliance issues. They are the best!" (emphasis added).

The second question applies to any type of therapy and measures the timeliness of receiving medication. Patients may obtain a prescription, but not onboard if they can't quickly and easily get the medication.

Timeliness matters to patients and their medical outcomes. One patient emphasizes this point: "I appreciate the fact that they call my doctor when I need a new prescription and *they make sure I get my medications on time*" (emphasis added).

Another patient noted: "They are great with contacting me before I need the next dose sent to my house. If I don't respond within a reasonable time, they follow up. *Meds have always been delivered on time*" (emphasis added).

Even though "logistical support" sounds a lot like common sense (which it is), it is *critical* for initial patient onboarding and adherence over time. It's hard to imagine a positive patient support services experience that doesn't include logistical support. In fact, logistical support is key to accessibility, and logistical experiences should be intentionally created with the same effort as financial assistance. What's the point of a patient being able to afford medication if it's too difficult to obtain? Get creative here—the range of possible transportation experiences is vast, and patient support services teams can create experiences that can surprise and delight patients. This is low-hanging fruit for creating an emotional bond with your customer.

LOGISTICAL SUPPORT BENCHMARKS

For rare disease medications, there is room to improve logistical support, as 40% of patients have difficulty finding their treatment location. This is unacceptable, and support teams must improve in this area.

On the other hand, approximately 80% of patients find the time it took to get the medication after getting their prescription to be "reasonable." That said, reasonable shouldn't be confused with fast. Often for rare diseases, it can take a month or longer to get the necessary approvals and scheduling in place to onboard patients, and there is little pharma companies can do to speed up that process. However, you do have the ability to keep patients informed throughout that approval process. We find that when they feel this way, they're more likely to feel their time to obtain their medication was reasonable since they understand *why* the process took the time it did.

"HOW DO I TAKE THIS DRUG?"

Once affordability and logistical support are fulfilled, patient support services' next area of focus is on helping patients with administering their new medication.

Once a patient is confident they can afford their medication and know where to obtain it, their next key need is administering the medication. Your patient support team should constantly ask themselves: *does the patient know how to administer their newly prescribed medication?*

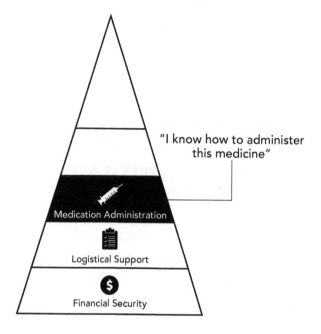

Patient Support Services Hierarchy of Needs

"I know how to administer this medicine"

Medication Administration

Logistical Support

Financial Security

We've found over and over again that if a patient can afford their new medication and knows how to get it, but is unsure how to administer it, they will not onboard.

This is an important yet nuanced area since patient support teams generally cannot advise patients on their medication or therapy. As such, you need to give your support team adequate resources and processes so that they can help patients answer their administration questions within the legal boundaries of what a patient support team can provide. Often, this means being able to direct patients to literature that can help them or to medical support lines, or transferring them directly to healthcare providers.

Even if your team is not tasked with explaining medication administration to the patient, the fact that you did not ignore the patient's needs will go a long way in terms of their experience. To measure the efficacy of patient support services for medication administration, our PeopleMetrics's model includes the following question that measures the medication administration need. It is asked on a 5-point agreement scale (5 = Strongly Agree, and 1 = Strongly Disagree):

1. The instruction materials I received on administering my medication were easy to understand.

For rare disease therapy, this is especially important. These medicines can be complex and difficult to administer. But even for less complex therapies, patients being sure that they know how they are supposed to administer their new medication—timing, amount, method, expiration—provides another level of comfort that they are on their way toward onboarding.

For certain medications, drug administration is paramount, and it may require adding questions to make sure you are fulfilling the key patient need of "I know how to administer this medication." For example, when it comes to infusion centers, which are important for many oncology and autoimmune treatments, understanding the patient experience—getting guidance on which center to visit, how to get there, and the experience with their first and subsequent infusions—is well worth the effort.

Even for relatively straightforward injections, there can be confusion. One PeopleMetrics client found that patients were unnecessarily refrigerating their medicine, causing pain during the injection. In this instance, listening to patients on real-world usage in real-time allowed the client to provide better clarity around storage and improve the patient experience.

Drug administration is also at the heart of treatments involving devices (e.g., CGMs, autoinjectors, etc.), and the experience patients have with these devices can make or break onboarding and adherence. Asking questions around the usability of the device is key.

And if your product is administered via a specialty pharmacy, questions around the customer experience there are key as well. Finally, if nurse educators are visiting patients in their homes to assist with medication administration (see Secret #3), it's a good idea to include a question in your survey to assess their effectiveness. If medication administration is extremely complex, adding nurse educators to the patient experience will provide a real boost. Again, the key is to create with intention the experiences that best fulfill the needs of your unique patient population. You have choices, but the worst one is to let patient experiences happen by chance instead of creating them intentionally.

Much like logistical support, medication administration seems like common sense, and it is. But many pharma companies continue to overlook the common sense wins that drive customer experience and are vital for initial patient onboarding and adherence over time.

Focus on your patient communications materials, over and over again! Make sure they are part of your digital patient engagement technology too and that your case managers (if you have them) are prepared to help in this area.

Test these communications via the various channels you have available before releasing them to patients. Once you are confident in these materials, continuously measuring their effectiveness and making changes based on feedback is what pharma CX is all about.

While most patients understand the instructional materials on administering their medication, we see comments like the ones below quite often.

- "[I would like] better help to *understand the side effects* of medications" (emphasis added).

- "[I want more] knowledge and advice *on medication use, side effects, and what to expect*" (emphasis added).
- "My representative is so kind and helpful. The only reason I didn't give the full ten stars is because I had a question about *timing around dosing, and he couldn't answer it*, which might be appropriate given his training there. He referred me to my pharmacist, who could only partially answer the question and referred me back to [the pharma company]. So, it would be good to have someone who can answer specific timing questions" (emphasis added).

HCPs who have patients with a rare disease also can get frustrated if medication administration is unclear. For example, one physician noted: "It is extremely nerve-racking, and you never really know what to expect. Mostly, it is fear of the unknown. I think it would really help if you provided videos or some sort of tutorial, PowerPoint, etc....Also, an explanation of what to expect after the infusion, such as side effects would be helpful...*It's just the little things that no one ever explains or takes the time to mention because they seem so minor.* Anyway, it really is the unknown of what to expect during and after the infusions" (emphasis added).

Taking time to make sure your patient support services team and case managers have clear processes and resources available to inform your customer about administering the medication is key. Training and a consistent process makes this happen if you have a call center approach or case managers. However, making sure your medication administration literature is clear and engaging is key as well. Videos, online tutorials, and the like are highly effective digital strategies to make sure you patients are administering their medication properly. The bottom line is, if you take medication administration for granted or assume that your patients already know how to do it, they may not onboard.

MEDICAL ADMINISTRATION BENCHMARKS

The good news is that most patients (88%) have a positive experience receiving instructional materials on administering their medication and feel the materials are easy to understand.

However, it is something that patient support teams need to be mindful of when building patient materials and case manager trainings. When we ask patients what they would improve about their support program, we hear patients looking for more information about administration and side effects. While these aren't topics support programs can assist with, as mentioned earlier, patients still expect support, so you need to be prepared to help patients find the answers they are looking for.

SECRET
#15

LOVE YOUR CUSTOMER

**Once the three fundamental patient needs
are fulfilled, patient support services
can add unique value to the patient
by providing a true support system.**

In this phase, you are moving beyond customer support and into true emotional connections that result in long-term customers and advocates for your company. Start with a system that helps patients easily get answers to their questions before they onboard onto their newly prescribed medication.

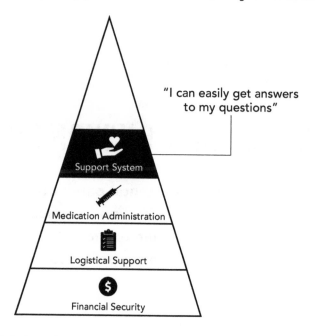

PeopleMetrics

Patient Support Services Hierarchy of Needs

"I can easily get answers
to my questions"

Support System

Medication Administration

Logistical Support

Financial Security

We know that supporting patients can be tricky given the numerous legal boundaries to what patient support services teams are permitted to discuss with patients. Patients aren't usually aware of these limitations, however, so your approach to answering these types of questions can have a significant impact on the patient experience (see example in Secret #4).

This is true if you have an in-house team or if you use a partner Hub, and it is especially important if the medication is for a rare disease. It's a huge responsibility and opportunity to add significant value.

When you think about how to create experiences to support this patient need, consistency is key. For the questions your team *can* answer, you need to make sure that everyone on your team provides *consistent* answers to each patient. For the questions you *cannot* answer, make sure that your team has a consistent process for directing patients to doctors, advocacy groups, or other resources that are able to further assist them.

While you cannot control what questions your team can and cannot answer, you can control the process by which your team responds to patient inquiries. Not only can it mean the difference between onboarding or not...it can and does change lives!

Unlike the past few patient needs, for which only one or two questions were required, providing a support system requires detailed feedback from patients about their experience.

Let's start with two questions that apply to any type of drug—from rare disease to mass-market medications:

1. *I have a clear understanding of the patient support services available.*

Awareness of the extent of support services offered is often the key to helping patients onboard.

One patient perfectly summed up what patient support services means to them: "*All the help I need* is a phone call away" (emphasis added).

The next question is about communication, which is fundamental for providing an effective patient support system:

2. *How would you describe the level of communication that you received from [insert company name] during your onboarding (including emails, mailings, and communications from your case manager)?*

   - *Not enough communication*
   - *Just the right amount*
   - *Too much communication*

You'll notice that we mention case managers in this question. If you have case managers, use this question as-is. If you don't have case managers, this question is still relevant. Getting your communication cadence correct builds the foundation of the support system you're providing for your patients.

HCPs especially appreciate just the right amount of communication from patient support services, given the number of patients they see. As one noted, "We have *frequent communication in our preferred method.* Communication/updates are timely" (emphasis added).

Another HCP said: "[My case manager] is always willing to help and is so supportive with whatever our clinic needs. She is *quick to respond and keeps great communication.* I couldn't ask for anyone better!" (emphasis added).

MEASURING CASE MANAGER PERFORMANCE

If you have case managers, you should ask a series of questions about patients' interactions with them. The first is answered on a 5-point scale (1 = Not at All Satisfied, and 5 = Extremely Satisfied):

1. *Please rate your satisfaction with your case manager, [insert case manager name].*

The next two questions dig into case manager performance:

2. *Based on your interaction with [insert case manager name], how strongly would you agree that your case manager provided you with accurate, up-to-date information?*

3. *Based on your interaction with [insert case manager name], how strongly would you agree that your case manager is accessible when you have questions or concerns?*

As the following quotes make clear, patients really appreciate having a case manager:

"[My case manager] is extremely informative, kind, and *helpful assisting me through this process.* I could not have received better customer service" (emphasis added).

"[My case manager] is always quick to respond. *[She] always answers questions* I may have, and if she doesn't know, she'll find a patient app for messaging non-urgent things. Overall [the pharma company] is so helpful and takes a huge weight off my shoulders" (emphasis added).

HCPs too. One HCP said: *"Very responsive, always follows up,* friendly, polite, organized, great with problem solving and troubleshooting when needed" (emphasis added).

Accuracy and timeliness of information provided by case managers is key to any effective patient support system. Patients also need to feel like they can count on being able to contact their case manager when they need to. A support system that isn't accessible won't be very effective.

One patient summarizes this perfectly. "It has always been easy to get a hold of a patient support member at [the pharma company]. They always have someone calling me to remind me to place our order or to ask how everything is going. Their team members are always so polite and nice. *I love that they talk to me as a person and not as a case number on a list. I have always had all my questions answered,* and everything is always very professional" (emphasis added).

An HCP adds, "I feel we get a lot of support from the patient support specialists assigned to our clinic. I find [my representatives] to be very helpful. *They respond to my questions and calls promptly*, which allows me to better care for our patients" (emphasis added).

An important point here is that hiring case managers does not guarantee an excellent patient experience. The patient experience with case managers still must be created with intention—hiring the right people, arming them with information they can share with patients, making sure case managers know where to refer patients for questions they cannot answer, and making case-manager access a priority.

After creating these experiences, measure case-manager performance consistently, make changes when necessary, enable case managers access to their results in real-time on a software platform like PeopleMetrics, and make sure you follow up with any patient who feels their case manager is difficult to reach.

QUESTIONS TO INFORM A DIFFERENTIATED PATIENT EXPERIENCE

The last two questions for this need focus on what your best case managers are doing to exceed patient expectations and provide a differentiated experience:

1. *Thinking of your interactions with [insert case manager name], was there a time when they exceeded your expectations?*

   ◦ *Yes*
   ◦ *No*

If the patient answers "Yes," they are asked this follow-up question:

2. *Please tell us specifically what they did.*

This question lets patients share in their own words what makes their case manager interactions special.

This is gold! And you might get comments like this one from patients:

"It is so nice to have a kind, responsive person to go to when you start something new and a bit scary. [My case manager] has always responded by email or called and talked to me on the phone. *He has explained things so well and has helped in many ways*" (emphasis added).

"[My case manager] is extremely informative, kind, and *helpful assisting me through this process*. I could not have received better customer service" (emphasis added).

Or consider these effusive case manager reviews from two HCPs: "SHE IS AMAZING! [My case manager] is *very patient-focused* and center-focused. She knows her job and she does it with ease. She's very compassionate and cares about the patients and the centers" (emphasis added).

"*Great customer service*, great responsiveness, *always going above and beyond* to help the care center as well as the patients and families" (emphasis added).

More importantly, feedback like this triggers the pharma CX feedback loop to begin again. With open-ended feedback, you can understand what makes a great case manager and how to deliver a patient experience that exceed expectations. You can identify what *all* case managers should be doing to make the patient experience the best it can be. You can create training material for new case managers based on patient feedback. After case managers are trained, continuous measurement allows you to access the impact of the training. And it shows you what to look for when hiring new case managers!

That is what will set you apart from the competition—a differentiated patient experience! You can even use this patient feedback to recognize your best case managers, which only incentivizes your team to continue their exceptional pharma CX work.

Please note that if you ask about case manager performance, your survey partner will need to be experienced in flagging patient comments about adverse events. While it is unlikely for patients to mention adverse events in response to this type of question, all patient comments need to be put through an adverse-events process (see Secret #20 for more on adverse-event reporting).

SUPPORT SYSTEM BENCHMARKS

Our benchmarks find that patients are struggling to understand what patient support services are offered. *Thirty percent of patients do not have a full understanding of these services.* This is an opportunity for pharma to engage with both HCPs and patients.

On the other hand, the communication provided to patients is rated highly in terms of the *amount* of information provided. We find that 80% believe they are receiving "just the right amount." Most patients are receiving the right amount of information, but the clarity of the communication can be improved.

We see consistently high scores from patients evaluating case managers. For example, more than *80% of patients are extremely satisfied with their case manager.* Moreover, almost all patients (over 90%) report that their case manager provides accurate information and is accessible. Finally, 70%

of patients report that their case manager did something that exceeded their expectations!

The impact of case managers is not to be underestimated. They have a profound impact on the patient experience. We see this repeatedly. Case manager importance has also been a key theme in this book. In fact, it's a secret in its own right—*to achieve the very best patient experience, use case managers to guide patients through their treatment journey.*

Providing an effective support system for patients is difficult and complex—but it's worth it, and here's why:

Once a patient feels they have a support system and can get answers to their questions, they move to the top of the pyramid—the ultimate patient need—confidence.

CONFIDENCE CHANGES EVERYTHING

The ultimate measure of the effectiveness of patient support services is patient confidence in onboarding onto new medications.

In recent years, pharma manufacturers have increasingly focused on providing support services to patients.

The goal of providing these services, either through an in-house team or a partner Hub, is to increase likelihood of patients onboarding to new medications and adhering over time.

PeopleMetrics

Patient Support Services Hierarchy of Needs

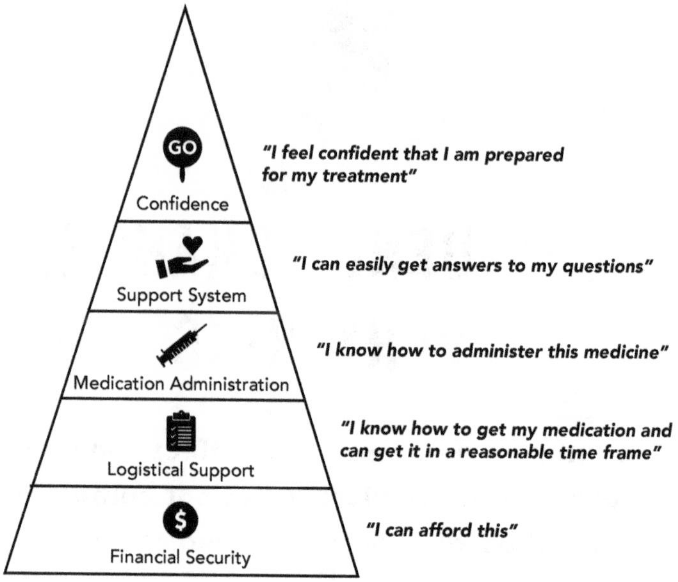
GO
Confidence
"I feel confident that I am prepared for my treatment"
Support System
"I can easily get answers to my questions"
Medication Administration
"I know how to administer this medicine"
Logistical Support
"I know how to get my medication and can get it in a reasonable time frame"
$
Financial Security
"I can afford this"

To do this, we move into the fifth and final level of patient need and Secret #16—*confidence.*

Patient Support Services Hierarchy of Needs

Is the patient confident they are prepared for treatment?

Is the patient confident that all their questions have been answered and they're ready to onboard?

This is why patient support services exist in the first place.

Fulfilling this need is an outcome of success on the previous four levels. If you intentionally create experiences that result in patients feeling that they can afford the medication, being able to access it, knowing how to administer it, and feeling supported in having their questions answered, confidence will follow.

Here's the bottom line from our work with thousands of patients—confident patients onboard. Patients who aren't confident might not. Do you want to take this risk? You don't have to if your patient support services deliver an exceptional patient experience!

MEASURING PATIENT CONFIDENCE

So, what's the best way to measure confidence?

In our model, we use *three questions* to measure patient confidence:

1. **Net Satisfaction Score (NSS)**

   "Net Satisfaction Score" asks patients how satisfied they are with the overall process of receiving their therapy. This question is answered on an 11-point scale (where 0 = Not at All Satisfied, and 10 = Extremely Satisfied).

   Responses to this question allow us to create segments of patients based on their overall satisfaction with services offered.

   Patients who answer 9 or 10 are considered Promoters. They are confident and ready to onboard. Patients who answer 7 or 8 are considered Passives. They are still likely to onboard but have outstanding concerns. Patients who answer 0 to 6 are Detractors. There is a real chance they will not onboard.

The NSS is calculated by subtracting detractors from promoters.

2. **Open-Ended Patient Comments**

Immediately after the net satisfaction question, we ask patients a follow-up open-ended question asking them to explain their answer.

Similar to the open-ended feedback on case managers in Secret #15, these patient comments are extremely valuable.

Since onboarding and support needs are different for each medication, open-ended feedback is critical for getting specific details on what patients find difficult about your process. The more specific you can be for each customer experience, the more supported each patient will feel, and the better retention your company will have.

But be careful—as with the open-ended question on case managers described in Secret #15, make sure your survey partner has an adverse-event reporting process in place. While it's rare for patients to share adverse events from their medication in this question, it does happen, and when it does, it must be reported immediately. More on this in our final secret, #20.

3. **Treatment Preparedness**

Confidence is more than just satisfaction, though. It also involves the patient feeling prepared to begin treatment. The final question we use to measure patient confidence addresses their preparedness.

A. *Do you feel that your experience with [insert company name] and [insert case manager name] has adequately prepared you to begin treatment?*

- *Yes*
- *No*

We originally asked this question as a 5-point agreement scale but found that the yes/no dichotomy gave us more reliable results.

This is the ultimate question to measure patient confidence and likelihood to onboard onto a new medication.

Patients who don't feel prepared for treatment usually have an outstanding issue within the first four levels of the Patient Hierarchy of Needs.

We have found those patients who answer "Yes" to the preparedness onboard 99% of the time, while patients who answer "No" to the treatment preparedness question only onboard 66% of the time!

This is so important to our pharma clients that most set up an alert to notify them immediately if a patient indicates that they are not prepared to begin treatment, allowing the client to "close the loop" with the patient.

CONFIDENCE BENCHMARKS

Let's begin with net satisfaction with patient support services. Our benchmark Net Satisfaction Score is 31.1. This is calculated by subtracting Detractors from Promoters. Passives are not included in the calculation of the Net Satisfaction Score, yet they are key to getting a higher NSS! A "7" or an "8" means the customer is close to being a Promoter, but there is something missing. The trick to moving a Passive to a Promoter is figuring out what is missing. How do you do that? Ask them. Using advanced survey logic, you can ask a follow-up question to only those customers who are Passives, asking what could be done for them to become "Extremely Satisfied" with the process of receiving their therapy.

Promoters for patient support services are about half of all patients surveyed (51%), while Detractors make up about 20%. In turn the Net Satisfaction Score is 31.1 (51.1–20).

To give this context, 31 is the middle of the road Net Promoter Score (NPS), with everyday brands like Home Depot and GEICO in this range. World class NPS scores are above seventy; iconic brands like Apple and Disney score in that range.

Pharma could do a better job with the overall patient-support experience. And they are paying the price for not yet doing so.

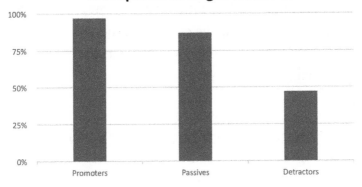

% Prepared to Begin Treatment

Among Detractors, only *49% felt prepared to begin treatment* and onboard onto their new medication.

Yes, you read that right. More than half of patients who had a poor experience with patient support services were not prepared to onboard onto their new medication.

But it changes quickly when the patient experience improves. Eighty-seven percent of Passives indicated they were prepared to begin treatment and onboard, as did 97% of Promoters!

The massive ROI of your investment in patient support services is plain as day. But it takes work. The pharma CX—intentional creation, continuous real-time measurement, and proactive management of experiences—makes it possible. And remember, this does not have to be daunting; I recommend starting small (see Secret #10).

In Secret #17, I will describe a tried-and-true technique for proactively managing the customer experience that will help turn around those Detractor patients who do not feel prepared to begin treatment.

CUSTOMER EXPERIENCE COMMENTS—PREPARED FOR TREATMENT

The patients who are prepared for treatment feel comfortable that their questions have been answered and appreciate the support team members (especially case managers) who have helped them.

- "She always makes sure *I feel secure in participating* in the program and my needs are being met" (emphasis added).
- "She is very professional in *making sure that I understand everything* and that she is available if I need anything answered" (emphasis added).
- "If there is anything I need to know or to be made aware of, she's on top of it. *I trust her*" (emphasis added).
- "*It is so nice to have a kind, responsive person to go to when you start something new and a bit scary.* [My representative] has always responded by email or called and talked to me on the phone. He has explained things so well and has helped in many ways" (emphasis added).
- "[My representative] is incredibly professional and polite. She possesses excellent interpersonal skills.

Her ability to assist in a timely and efficient manner is beyond satisfactory. Her willingness *to assist and resolve any issue has far exceeded my expectations*" (emphasis added).

CUSTOMER EXPERIENCE COMMENTS—*NOT* PREPARED FOR TREATMENT

Patients who do not feel prepared for treatment have questions that remain unanswered, not all of which patient support services are legally permitted to answer. However, the pharma CX mindset would lead patient support teams to create an experience that connects patients with third parties who can answer all their questions.

- "My representative is so kind and helpful. The only reason I didn't give the full ten stars is because *I had a question about timing around dosing and he couldn't answer it*, which might be appropriate given his training there. He referred me to my pharmacist, who could only partially answer the question and referred me back to [the pharma company]. *So, it would be good to have someone who can answer specific timing questions*" (emphasis added).
- "There still seems to be specific information not yet known about long term effects. *It would [be nice] to access a user database where information about effects can be updated.* It would be nice for people with [my

disease] [to be able to] read about new approaches to managing the disease" (emphasis added).

- *"I have questions regarding [my medication]*—[since] the protein being interrupted has other functions...does this interruption cause any side effects? I understand I should consult with my doctor on this, and I will, but I communicate more with you" (emphasis added).

PREPARING PATIENTS FOR TREATMENT IS JOB NUMBER ONE OF PATIENT SUPPORT SERVICES

Here are a few actions pharma can take to give patients the best chance of being prepared for treatment:

1. Generate awareness for patient support services. Simply offering these services to customers gives the patient a much-improved chance of being prepared. Patients and HCPs truly appreciate the support. However, awareness of patient support services can be a challenge. Based on our client conversations, it is often difficult to get marketing dollars for patient support services. Ensuring that sales representatives talk about patient support programs with the offices they visit goes a long way to generating awareness.

2. Provide case managers if appropriate. Patients love case managers. They answer their questions, provide emotional support, and are a trusted resource that patients

can rely on. Clearly not every therapy can have case managers, but if you do offer a rare disease drug, these are a must-have to getting every patient (from likely a small patient population) prepared for treatment.

3. Adopt the Patient Hierarchy of Needs no matter how complex your drug. The model shared in this book provides a roadmap on getting patients to a point where they feel prepared for treatment and onboarding. The model is comprehensive, each level counts, and you cannot skip steps. No matter how large or small your patient population, this model identifies the key patient needs you must fulfill to prepare them for treatment. For rare disease therapies, the focus on the patient needs at each level seems obvious. However, even for mass-market and less complex medications, each patient need must be fulfilled for patients to onboard and adhere over time. For example, consider a less complex drug that is delivered by an inhaler. In most cases, pharma will focus almost exclusively on access. There often is not a lot of support after initial access because the medication is widely accessible and not complex. Yet, while patients may easily get access and initially onboard, there is often a drop in long-term adherence. So, while financial security, logistical support, and administration may not be an issue, it's the support need that often goes unfulfilled. Patients need a support system no matter how straightforward it is to

gain access to the medication. This support can be delivered digitally, but it must be provided. The bottom line is if any of the patient needs in this model are missing, patients are unlikely to feel prepared and are at risk for not onboarding or not adhering over time.

CLOSE THE LOOP

Following up on poor experiences is the hallmark of experience management (e.g., pharma CX) and will increase patient onboarding.

As pointed out in Secret #3, hotels are the pioneers of measuring and constantly improving the customer experience. After all, a hotel's product *is* the experience!

The best hotel CX programs proactively manage the customer experience by following up when a guest indicates in a survey that they had a poor experience during a recent visit.

The reason for "closing the loop" with a guest is clear: *a guest with an unresolved issue is unlikely to return and likely to tell others about their poor experience on sites like TripAd-visor, Google Reviews, and Yelp.*

Should patient support services teams do the same and follow up when a patient or HCP has a bad experience?

Most definitely *yes*!

PROACTIVELY RESPONDING TO NEGATIVE EXPERIENCES

A key question in our Patient Hierarchy of Needs model is whether a patient feels "prepared" to begin treatment. It's a critical outcome to any patient support services offering and one that strongly links to successful onboarding and adherence over time.

This is a simple yes or no question—either a patient feels they are prepared, or they don't.

If a patient indicates that they do *not* feel prepared to begin treatment, an email alert is sent to designated people within the patient support services team and workflows are in place to ensure that the right person quickly follows up with the patient to resolve any issues.

We also recommend an alert be triggered on the overall satisfaction with patient services question that results in the Net Satisfaction Score (remember our Net Satisfaction benchmark was only 31.1 for patient support services, well below world-class levels of 60 or above).

Preparedness for treatment and Net Satisfaction Score are key "outcome" questions in our model. This means that they are the questions that link to patient behavior. In this case, the overall experience with patient support services (Net Satisfaction) drives preparedness, which in turn impacts likelihood to onboard.

This is one place where our clients get major, immediate value from our pharma CX programs. Have you ever had a patient reach out to you directly to tell you that they aren't ready for their treatment? Many of our clients experience this for the first time. The reason is that most are implementing their first pharma CX program. Previously, they had done market research studies, which do not reveal individual response data (see Secret #2). Now, you have an opportunity to solve patient onboarding and adherence issues that you never would have known about. Acting on each negative experience is critical!

PERSONAL IDENTIFIABLE INFORMATION (PII)

You may be asking yourself: how can we follow up with a patient after a poor experience and maintain our PII mandates?

Here is how this works. In the alert that is triggered based on either a lack of preparedness to begin treatment or a Detractor score, a unique patient identifier is the only information shared. This maintains patient confidentiality and keep PII secure.

It's important that you choose a survey partner that knows how to handle PII (see Secret #20). Surveying patients enrolled in your programs means that you have permission to contact them directly via email or SMS to send them a survey (see Secret #18). So, PII is always involved.

Here is a step-by-step process for protecting PII while closing the loop:

1. Send required PII data to your pharma CX partner along with whatever internal patient identifier your organization uses. This is commonly an individual code, such as a national provider identifier (NPI) number for HCPs.

2. With the PII, your pharma CX partner can send the survey and personalize their outreach with information like the patient's name and medication, which increases their likelihood to respond, benefiting the feedback program (see Secret #18 for more details).

3. When your pharma CX partner provides you with respondent data, they should remove all PII and only

identify survey respondents by their unique patient ID or NPI number. That way, you can be certain that sensitive patient or HCP information will not be seen. However, if there is a need to follow up with an individual patient or HCP, those with the appropriate permissions will be able to do so using the unique identifier (patient ID, NPI number).

WHAT ABOUT HUBS AND "CLOSING THE LOOP"?

Now you may be saying to yourself, "We are using a partner Hub to deliver our patient support services, so I don't have to worry about this..."

But you *do*—possibly even more so than if you were delivering patient support services in-house. Your partner Hub is representing *your* company. Patients often do not notice or even care who is delivering support services to them. All they care about is whether the service is poor. If it is, they won't onboard.

And that's your issue.

So, even if a bad experience is caused by a Hub partner, it's critical that there is complete transparency and a process in place for following up; this will yield significant ROI by increasing onboarding and adherence!

PHARMA CX IMPLEMENTATION SECRETS

HAVE FEEDBACK YOUR WAY

The most effective pharma CX programs collect feedback from patients, HCPs, and caregivers the way they want to provide it.

This secret focuses on the best methods to continuously measure patient, HCP, and caregiver feedback. There are four data collection methodologies for you to consider. Choosing the method that your customer is most comfortable using to provide feedback can make or break your pharma CX program. Make sure you are working with an external pharma CX partner who has experience with all these methods and understands which one is appropriate for your unique patient or HCP population (see Secret #20 for more on external pharma CX partners).

USE GENERIC SURVEY LINKS

Sometimes the most effective methodology is also the simplest. The beauty of the generic survey link lies in its flexibility and speed to market. A generic survey link is a unique URL that directs a potential respondent directly to a digital survey where they can provide feedback.

The generic link survey response is usually not tied to any type of operational or patient data (e.g., time on therapy, what drug they're taking, associated case manager, the site at which they are receiving treatment, etc.).

They are still able to capture valuable feedback at key moments of truth. For example, they can be shared on physical and digital marketing materials, emailed (marketing opted-in) to patients after a key touchpoint, shared with patients in person on a kiosk or iPad, embedded into an online patient portal, converted into a QR code, and more.

Generic survey links also provide patients and caregivers who may not have internet access the opportunity to provide feedback while they're at a physical location receiving treatment. Often, an iPad is used.

Consider using generic survey links if:

1. You have a complicated IT landscape (e.g., you're collecting feedback across many clinical trial sites

worldwide, or you do not have a readily available list of marketing-consented patients or HCPs).

2. A third party owns patient data (e.g., pharma company/ sponsor cannot reach out directly).

3. You need flexibility to distribute (e.g., on marketing materials, embedded within a patient portal, on an iPad).

For example, a multinational pharma client of ours wanted to collect feedback from a diverse patient population participating in an ongoing clinical trial. The pharma sponsor did not have access to patient contact information and could not meet the need for technical integrations with hundreds of clinical trial sites. This required a simple solution and not a heavy IT burden. A generic link was chosen. The survey was designed, programmed, and distributed on marketing and educational materials using a generic link. The generic link survey was also added to the company's patient portal. The survey collected feedback on the patient experience before, during, and after the trial to improve design, execution, and recruitment strategy for future clinical trials.

SEND EMAIL SURVEYS

For pharma companies looking for a best-in-class approach to continuous real-time measurement, automated email surveys provide immense value.

Automated email surveys are triggered off an experience the patient or HCP has with your company. The transaction is logged, the patient/HCP sample (customer list) generated, and the email survey sent. In the email, customers find a link, usually with a unique identifier at the end, that appends additional information about the respondent.

There are three primary advantages to this approach:

1. **Ease of use.** Email surveys allow customers to receive and respond on their own time, which has a positive impact on response rates. Instead of limiting a patient to responding immediately after a phone call (IVR) or after spending hours at a facility receiving treatment (e.g., generic survey link on an iPad), patients can provide feedback about their experience in the comfort of their own home and on their own time.

2. **Linking operational and organizational data.** Email surveys provide a unique opportunity to seamlessly link operational and organizational data to survey responses. Insights do not begin and end with survey responses; you can tie internal data to an individual respondent's feedback to understand the customer experience much more deeply. Want to see how overall patient satisfaction is trending? Want to cut it by case manager? Want to know how the patient experience changed after you launched a new disease state education program? The

screenshot below gives a sense of how tying organizational data—specifically the assigned case manager—to patient feedback can enrich your analysis. Tying operational and organizational data to patient or HCP feedback allows you to get to these and other insights.

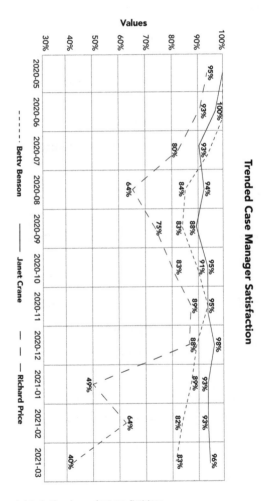

All names and data in the above chart are fictitious.

3. **Personalized invitations and targeted reminders increase response rates.** Finally, with an email survey tied to a unique identifier, you will know exactly who has completed the survey and who has not. This allows you to personalize the email invitation with the customer name, when they interact with your team, and more, thereby boosting response rates. This allows you to send targeted reminders to customers who have not completed the survey, and to send a thank you email to those who have. Response rates for email surveys in pharma CX range from 10% to up to 30% depending on the type of therapy and patient population.

Email surveys are the best choice if:

1. You have a list of marketing-consented patients or HCPs with email addresses.

2. The goal of the program is to enrich customer feedback with operational and organizational data to get to the core issues impacting the customer experience.

3. You require higher response rates (e.g., limited patient population for rare disease medication).

LEVERAGE SMS CHANNELS

SMS or text surveys are becoming increasingly popular.

They offer many of the advantages of email surveys with the added benefit of increased response rates thanks to the popularity of texting. The most effective SMS approach is sending a link with a unique identifier to a patient or HCP via text similar to the email survey approach described above.

The other version is called two-way SMS, which allows you to have a conversation, sending and receiving text and multimedia messages. This enables a case manager to chat with a patient and allows surveys to be responsive to the answers a patient provides. This requires more of a back-and-forth with the customer (patient, HCP) and can limit the quantity and quality of feedback you receive.

The challenge with SMS is getting permission from your customers to send them a text message in the first place. It's another level of marketing consent but can be well worth the investment. Keep in mind that data charges can still be applied to texts you send to patients or HCPs, so obtaining permission to send texts is required.

Twilio is a good place to begin for SMS surveys. They are a leading cloud service provider that uses an application programming interface (API) to send and receive text messages. The data flow is essentially the same as with other methodologies we work with. PeopleMetrics receives the customer transactional data from the pharma company or partner Hub, then sends the data to Twilio with a unique identifier, and Twilio texts the customer the invitation text and survey link.

Text surveys are the best choice if:

1. You have a list of marketing-consented patients or HCPs with texting information.

2. You need the highest levels of response rates and engagement from customers.

3. Your pharma CX partner can embed a survey link within a text through third parties such as Twilio or Open-Market.

Text messages garner more attention from customers than other data collection methods. Your response rates will go up—sometimes a lot (over a 30% survey response rate based on our client data). However, text surveys are a long game. It will require a deliberate effort to collect this information, get permission to send texts to your customers, and find a survey partner who is adept at coordinating it all (see Secret #20).

TRY INTERACTIVE VOICE RESPONSE (IVR) SURVEYS

Some situations, or moments of truth, may require continuous measurement of the customer experience with a guaranteed high response rate. In these cases, Interactive Voice Response (IVR) is an option to consider.

IVR is good for measuring an experience immediately after a call with a contact center or case manager. It's very easy for the patient to stay on the line and answer a few questions. For that reason, IVR tends to have the highest response rates of any of the methodologies (over 50%). Many pharma companies have a team of case managers who support patients with access services, financial support, disease state, administration education, and more. Whether these services are internal or routed through a HUB, a transactional IVR survey can capture valuable in-the-moment feedback on a patient's recent experience.

How does it work? First, IVR integrates into your company's internal phone system. Before a call is connected, the patient or HCP will be asked if they would like to stay on the line to provide feedback on their experience once the call ends. If they say yes, they have consented to participating in the IVR survey. For example, once a call with a case manager ends, the patient is transferred to the IVR survey and given the option to answer a series of questions about their experience. This process can be automated (e.g., the consenting patient is automatically transferred without the case manager initiating) or non-automated (e.g., the case manager must connect the patient to the survey manually).

If your technical landscape permits, an automated IVR survey program is your best option. By automating your IVR feedback program, you're controlling for a major variable that could adversely impact the integrity of your data: case manager or agent bias.

In non-automated programs, the case manager or agent manually transfers consenting patients to the IVR survey upon completing the call. In this case, a case manager could choose *not* to transfer a patient after a call goes poorly. Controlling for this type of bias is critical for the integrity of data and the strategy it informs.

When the call is completed, the feedback is automatically uploaded into a real-time software platform (like PeopleMetrics).

The downside of IVR surveys is that they are generally limited to having between three and five questions due to the need for each question to be read verbally to the customer. Another disadvantage is that open-ended comments can be cumbersome for customers to provide.

The good news is system integrations can associate customer information (e.g., unique identifier for PII), operational data (e.g., high/low prescribing physician), and organizational data (e.g., case manager name) to the IVR survey response. This allows you to analyze responses with advanced segmentation for added insights.

IVR is the best choice if:

1. Telephone conversations between patients/HCPs and case managers occur regularly.

2. In-depth questioning and open-ended feedback are not a part of your program goals.

3. Feedback needs to be given as close to the "moment of truth" as possible, and you want high response rates.

4. The patient population would respond better to telephone technology (given factors like age, disease state) and/or they likely don't have access to the internet or smart devices.

For example, a US-based pharma company in the rare disease space was launching its first approved product. With an extremely small patient population, measuring the patient experience is tricky and each voice is extremely valuable. For this company, the interaction between the patient and case manager was a priority.

Immediately after specific telephone interactions, patients

who consented to provide feedback were directed to an IVR survey, and the feedback was used to improve future interactions and coach case managers to better support future patients.

The pharma company was able to begin collecting topline data in less than a month and work toward patient-centricity.

MIXED METHODOLOGY CAN ANSWER COMPLEX PROBLEMS

Sometimes the right answer isn't any single methodology. A core principle of the customer experience industry (and the emerging pharma CX industry) is meeting your customer (or in this case, patient, HCP, caregiver) where they are—or where they're most likely to provide feedback.

For example, if you want to track the patient experience across the entire treatment journey, it will be most impactful to trigger an email or SMS survey after a patient hits a key milestone. Then, you can tie that feedback to operational, organizational, and (de-identified) patient information. This allows you to get to the heart of the insights that drive value for patients across the treatment journey.

If you're also interested in collecting feedback from patients about their experience at a treatment center, it would make more sense to execute on an iPad or kiosk with a generic link.

Finally, if you want to round out the program with a call center survey for when a patient calls in for support with treatment information, logistical questions, billing concerns, and more, transferring the patient directly to an IVR phone survey while the interaction is still fresh in their mind makes a lot of sense.

RESPONSE RATES

In general, you will get the highest response rates when you place the least burden on the customer. The choice of data collection methodology will have an impact on response rates, but so will survey length, the mobile friendliness of the survey, the clarity of the messaging around the survey, and more.

IVR has the highest response rates because it is easy for a respondent to stay on the phone after a support call and answer just a few questions. You can obtain response rates as high as 70% with IVR, with most falling in the range of 40–50%. Email and SMS will often get you good response rates with much more information than IVR can. We have seen response rates as high as 30% using these methods, with most falling between 10% and 15%. Generic link response rates depend on external factors such as how much time a respondent has to fill out a survey on the spot, the communication around the importance of providing feedback, and, if an iPad is being used, whether it's available to multiple patients at a time. These response rates range from very low (3–5%) to quite high (over 40%) depending on these factors.

GETTING IT RIGHT

The goals of your program, current IT landscape, and the unique characteristics of your patient population will ultimately determine the methodology and channel(s) you employ to collect customer feedback. Be sure to consider your patients' disease states when choosing both a survey method and invitation timing.

Working with an experienced partner to help you design your pharma CX program can help you navigate the nuances of collecting patient feedback in a highly regulated industry like pharma. More on this in Secret #20.

	Generic Link	Email Link	Text	IVR
Have Marketing-Consented Customer List		X	X	
Onsite Feedback	X			
Immediate Feedback Post-Call				X
Link to Operational / Organizational Data		X	X	X
Open-Ended Feedback	X	X	X	
Set Up Quickly	X			X
Highest Response Rates				X
Personalized Survey Invitation		X		
Ensure Anonymity	X			
Send Targeted Reminders		X		
Include in Marketing Materials	X			

DON'T GO IT ALONE

Pharma CX requires a village (or at least a team of internal champions).

Who is going to help you build buy-in and implement your pharma CX program?

In many ways, the *who* is even more important than the *how*. Without the right players, your pharma CX program will not get off the ground. In this secret, I focus on the key internal stakeholders within your organization whom you need to include to create experiences with intention, measure these experiences continuously, and manage them proactively.

START WITH THE PATIENT SERVICES TEAM

Your patient services team has an intimate understanding of the important interactions patients have with your company. They can identify the treatment milestones that are moments of truth, and they understand common patient questions and concerns. These team members can help imagine and create the best experiences possible for patients using support services.

Patient services team members also serve as key points of contact during program implementation, help finalize the touchpoints to collect patient feedback, follow up with patients who report bad experiences or are at risk of non-adherence, and more!

This team may be leading the pharma CX effort in patient support services or partnering with a customer experience lead within Pharma Corporate or a member of the brand insights team. In any event, if pharma CX is focused on patient support services, they are a vital team to include.

ADD A CLINICAL TEAM

If your pharma CX program focuses on the clinical side, make sure your global clinical trial leaders are first creating the best experience possible for clinical trial patients, and then incorporating patient feedback as a part of your study protocols. Clinical pharma CX partners like PeopleMetrics (see Secret #20) and proven survey tools like TransCelerate have streamlined the process. Incorporating survey approvals into your trial design is more seamless than ever before!

After getting the survey included, the next step is communicating the purpose and expectations of the survey to your various trial sites. Since patient surveys are relatively new in the clinical field, it's important to communicate to your stakeholders the importance of patient feedback in improving the clinical trial experience.

These stakeholders will include CROs, country managers, clinical site managers, and site staff. Each member of the team should be aware of the survey so they can respond to patient questions. Your clinical teams should be able to communicate the purpose and value of these surveys to patients to increase response rate. Prepare them for these questions by giving them an overview of and reminders about the survey in your clinical trial meetings, newsletters, and regular site communications.

INCLUDE MARKET RESEARCH/INSIGHTS

Market research (sometimes called Insights) is different from pharma CX (see Secret #2), but market research professionals are critical to a successful pharma CX program. Market research often has input into the design of the survey instrument and can help drive actionable insights through analysis and reporting. They are a trusted advisor to make sure you are asking the right questions to the right audience at the right time via the right data collection method (see Secret #18).

And you may be able to return the favor! Market researchers may want to insert "hot-swap" questions into your continuous measurement programs. "Hot swap" questions are market research questions temporarily inserted into an ongoing pharma CX program. For example, a market researcher might want to understand patient awareness and understanding of new messaging being used in marketing materials. Message-testing questions can be inserted into your continuous patient support services onboarding survey. Once a certain number of completed surveys are obtained, the questions can be removed and swapped with new survey questions.

Market researchers are your friends. And over time, pharma CX and market research are likely to converge as "hot swap"-type opportunities emerge.

THE ROLE OF INFORMATION TECHNOLOGY (IT)

To make pharma CX happen, you need IT to be your friend. They are vital in the technical lift involved with a pharma CX program. IT helps estimate the internal scope of work for system integrations, evaluates (and confirms) the data security protocols of your survey partner, and leads technical system integrations.

IT controls the most up-to-date information about the patient and HCP experience. The minimum support you need from IT is something called a *flat file*. This is often an Excel or CSV file that contains a list of patients or HCPs who recently had an experience with your company. Once you specify how frequently you need this information to be collected, IT can help you set up a process whereby you can upload the customer information into your survey partner's software platform so surveys can be sent out. IT can also help you create an automated system for this process, such as connecting a CRM to the survey software platform via an API.

INVOLVE LEGAL AND PROCUREMENT

Involving legal early and often will save you time and headaches throughout the implementation of your pharma CX program. A key responsibility of legal is reviewing the questions that get asked to patients or HCPs. Note that all questions in PeopleMetrics's Patient Hierarchy of Needs model (see Secrets #11–16) have been approved by multiple pharma legal teams.

Legal also ensures compliance with all legal and regulatory statutes, enforces standards for collecting data containing PII, and works with procurement and survey partners to finalize contracts.

A related department, procurement, may also get involved if you decide to go out to "bid" for a pharma CX program.

This group will help you craft a Response for Proposal (RFP) you can send out to multiple providers. Procurement will help you ask the right questions, consolidate responses, choose the right partner, and negotiate the cost/terms of the program.

RECRUIT AN EXECUTIVE SPONSOR

As noted in Secret #1, pharma CX is an organizational mindset, and leadership buy-in is required for true patient-centricity. A highly engaged executive sponsor will help guide the strategic vision of your pharma CX program, build buy-in across the organization, and most importantly, fund the program.

Nothing happens until somebody pays, and a strong executive sponsor will act as a liaison, facilitating collaboration amongst the cross-functional team of stakeholders.

FIND THOUGHTFUL PARTNERS

Pharma CX requires external partners—choose carefully.

There is one final *who* to consider—an experienced external pharma CX partner.

An external partner who has experience with pharma CX is invaluable. In particular, the right external partner can help you avoid common pitfalls and launch a successful pharma CX program quickly.

Did you hire your pharma CX external partner so that you could design your own surveys, figure out when and how to send the surveys, analyze the data yourself, and then figure out how to make the feedback actionable? Probably not.

Let's look at the key characteristics you should be looking for in an external partner.

PHARMA CX EXPERTISE

The first criterion is obvious: your partner needs experience and expertise in pharma CX. That is, you need to be confident they can help you map the journey of your customers, identify moments of truth, brainstorm the experiences you are going to intentionally create at these moments, continuously measure customer feedback in real-time, and provide software to help you proactively manage these experiences throughout the organization. The best pharma CX partners also help you regularly analyze results and make recommendations on how to improve the customer experience.

If your potential pharma CX external partner is focused on software licenses rather than helping you improve the experiences of our customers, run away!

Here are a handful of questions you can ask to better understand a prospective partner's pharma CX expertise:

1. Do you help map the customer journey?

2. What moments of truth have you found in other pharma CX programs?

3. Do you have best practice questions and benchmarks directly related to pharma CX (e.g., clinical, patient support services)?

4. Can additional questions specific to our company and unique patient population be included?

5. What are the response rates in your programs?

6. What feedback methodology do you recommend for my particular patient and HCP populations?

7. Do you have your own software that provides real-time results of customer feedback, including dashboards, case management, and text analytics?

8. Do you provide analysis, reporting, and recommendations?

9. What is your adverse-event reporting process?

You are the pharma expert, but your external partner should complement your expertise with capabilities around pharma CX. Do not settle!

DATA SECURITY PROTOCOLS

If you're evaluating a prospective partner who isn't HIPAA

compliant and doesn't have strong data security protocols in place, it's a nonstarter. At a minimum, ask for documentation on:

1. HIPAA Compliance

2. Soc 2 Data Security

3. GDPR Compliance

4. Internal Data Handling & Security Protocols

These items are the price of admission to play in the pharma CX space and should be relatively easy for the right external partner to demonstrate to you or your IT team.

ADVERSE-EVENT REPORTING CAPABILITIES

Any patient comment that references an adverse event resulting from their current medication must be flagged and reported. Your external partner should have specific people within their organization trained in adverse-event reporting, have experience flagging comments around adverse events, and have a process for reporting them.

The best practice in adverse-event reporting starts before you even collect any feedback; it starts with how you word your pharma CX surveys. Patient surveys for support teams and clinical trials are not supposed to be about their medical experience, so you should not ask questions that encourage patients to provide feedback regarding adverse events. With appropriate question wording, you can make sure you minimize the number of adverse-event reports that you collect. Adverse events usually make up fewer than 1% of feedback collected in pharma CX surveys.

Once you are fielding your survey, make sure that you're working with a survey partner who can review your full survey response volume daily and set up to communicate any adverse events to your pharmacovigilance teams.

The benefit of working with an experienced partner who reviews for adverse events daily is that your team can focus on acting on your patient feedback rather than responding to adverse events. For example, when our clients receive an alert that includes an adverse event, they can start following up with the patient knowing that their survey provider is handling the adverse event.

HEALTHCARE EXPERTISE

Any pharma CX external partner should know your space and have experience working with other pharma companies. If you have to hand-hold your partner through every step of the process, it will adversely impact project timelines (and likely your sanity).

Choose a partner who speaks your language and has experience working in the complicated regulatory environment of the pharma industry. If they're not intimately familiar with the challenges that a patient support services or clinical professional faces, look elsewhere.

PROPRIETARY SOFTWARE WITH REAL-TIME REPORTING

Patient and HCP feedback is exponentially more valuable if it can be accessed in real-time. This makes a real-time reporting software platform a must-have. A monthly Excel readout or PowerPoint report is not enough to proactively manage and improve the customer experience.

Your real-time reporting platform should be proprietary to your external partner and not licensed or "white labeled" from another firm. The reason is your partner should be able to accommodate your particular needs from a software development perspective. And your needs should get priority into the product roadmap.

The software platform should have the flexibility to see aggregate patient and HCP feedback across your company's full portfolio in real-time and also make it possible to immediately view and act on any individual response (while incorporating PII). The platform should provide robust analytics and unique data cuts to get at the core drivers of a great customer experience.

For example, if you have case managers responsible for supporting patients in specific regions, you should be able to view performance in aggregate, but also look at case manager performance by geography, by team, or by individual case manager:

Aggregate Case Manager Performance View

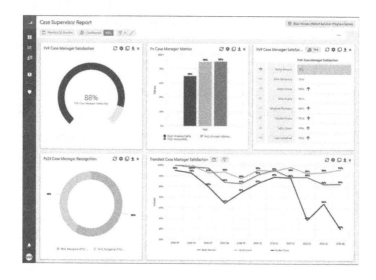

Individual Case Manager Performance View

Another example: if you collect data on insurance providers, you should be able to view overall satisfaction cut by insurance provider, treatment location, medication, or any other piece of data that you collect without limitation.

SIZE AND AGILITY

How many times have you been close to finalizing approvals from disparate stakeholders on a marketing communication or a questionnaire, when one stakeholder comes in at the eleventh hour to change a word or question, forcing you to start the process all over again?

Unfortunately, it happens. Working with a pharma CX

partner that is the right size, with the necessary internal processes to move quickly when changes are made, will go a long way toward adhering to project timelines.

At a minimum, you should demand a dedicated project manager who is intimately familiar with your program, has pharma CX expertise, operates as an extension of your team, and is available when you need them. There is no reason you should struggle to get a hold of your project manager when it comes time to make changes or have a question.

WE'RE IN THE FIRST INNING

The secrets in this book are only the beginning; there are opportunities to extend pharma CX to better understand and proactively manage the full patient journey.

It's common to hear that healthcare is the next frontier for the customer experience. My view is that pharma has the largest opportunity in the healthcare arena to impact patients' lives through better experiences.

There is a lot to learn from how CX leaders in other industries have gotten closer to the customer and created strong, emotional bonds. It is important for pharma to apply lessons learned.

Although pharma faces regulatory barriers that traditional CX leaders do not, the opportunity to create experiences for their customers—patients and HCPs—that are not only memorable but can extend and save lives is incredibly important. In fact, it is far more important than, say, a more comfortable stay for a guest at a hotel.

The purpose of this book was to challenge pharma leaders to think differently about their business. To think beyond products to experiences. To change their mindset. As a result, the secrets in this book were primarily focused on two experiences that pharma can immediately impact—the clinical trial experience and the commercial patient support services experience. There is so much work to do in these two areas, I decided this was an appropriate place to begin.

However, managing the full patient journey goes beyond these touchpoints. For example, consider patient interactions with HCPs. Does pharma control these interactions? No. Do they need to know about them and make the patient journey a better overall experience? Absolutely! How about HCP direct interactions with pharma, either through sales reps, digital engagement technologies, or conferences/symposia? All these experiences can be created with intention, continuously measured, and proactively managed!

There can be a reluctance at pharma companies to embrace pharma CX. What's required is a fundamental change in mindset, and for an industry as successful and impactful as pharma, change is hard. But it's necessary. And pharma's incredible speed and agility in creating multiple vaccines to combat a worldwide pandemic proves the industry more than has it in them!

You may hear objections such as, "We don't want to hear about any experiences that we don't own," or "That's not our department." That mindset can come from a reaction to regulatory overzealousness, aversion to risk, or a reluctance to cause a potential stir by collecting negative feedback. You should look to break this mindset down, as there is a real risk to not embracing pharma CX.

The truth is, by the time patients reach your clinical trial or your patient support team, they have been through a tremendous amount of stress, and you have the opportunity to lessen their burden. Taking care to support the patients you rely on goes a long way toward forming the emotional connection necessary to attract and keep customers.

Patient support teams face challenges to the patient experience beyond what has been covered in this book. How is the patient's experience with their HCP? How is their pharmacy experience? Are they satisfied with third-party patient advocacy networks that they participate in? Are they participating and getting value from patient events run by other teams? Are nurse educators giving them proper assistance and education on their therapy? What experiences do underserved populations expect, and how do we deliver these to them?

Moreover, to get true real-time feedback on the patient experience in patient support services, pharma needs to look beyond surveys. Needs assessments are becoming popular, which are shorter, more conversational, and happening at the touchpoints the staff has with patients. As this data from patients is gathered, they are entered into a CRM, enabling pharma to tailor future experiences to the individual patient.

All these experiences are points in the patient journey at which a patient can have a poor experience, and they may reach out to their support services team for assistance with these issues. Patients do not have a detailed understanding of who owns each of these interactions They generally see their support services team as broadly able to help them with their needs. So, if they have an issue along their patient journey and all they hear from their support team is "We don't deal with that" or "That's not us," they feel unsupported, which puts them at risk of improper adherence.

The more your patient support services teams know about the full patient journey, the better they can serve the patient. Pharma companies should ask why patient support teams are often isolated physically from the brand teams with which they're expected to work. A tighter integration between these teams will result in a better experience for the customer (with, of course, the appropriate data firewalls and regulatory compliance).

WE ARE ALL IN THIS TOGETHER. DON'T HESITATE TO REACH OUT!

We are at the very beginning of pharma's journey into creating, measuring, and managing the experiences of their customers. The pharma clients we work with are beginning to think of experiences rather than just products, as is the industry at large.

No one has this completely figured out, and we are all in this together. I am inspired daily by the courage of our pharma clients to rethink how they can better serve their customers, and I hope there is something in here that inspires you to create better experiences for your patients.

I am so excited that pharma is embarking on this journey!

If you're ready to take the next step to improve your pharma CX, and we can be of service to you or your organization in any way, please reach out. My contact information is below, along with a contact number for PeopleMetrics.

We've also got great resources for you to learn more. Our

blog has been recognized as one of the top in CX. You can subscribe by heading here:

https://www.peoplemetrics.com/px-blog#/

I also host a live webinar every two weeks on Tuesdays at 2:00 p.m. (EST) called PeopleMetrics Live! I encourage you to join us as we do a deep dive into CX and pharma CX topics.

Thank you for taking the time to read this book and learn more about pharma CX. I wish you all the best in your journey toward patient-centricity and creating exceptional experiences for your customers!

Sean McDade, PhD

Founder and CEO, PeopleMetrics

E-mail: sean.mcdade@peoplemetrics.com or info@peoplemetrics.com

Phone: 215.979.8030

ACKNOWLEDGMENTS

This book would not have been possible without my talented colleagues at PeopleMetrics. In particular, Kirk Lohbauer made immense contributions to this book: including client stories, clarifying technical language, and adding context that made the book so much better! Kirk, you know pharma CX at least as well as I do, probably better. You are a pioneer in pharma CX, and I am so glad you are on my team!

The entire customer experience team at PeopleMetrics helped in this effort, including Audrey Squaresky, Courtney Prunchak, and Jean Burns. Audrey, thank you for reading many drafts of the manuscript, always doing a great job, and never complaining! Courtney, your detailed comments on an early draft were so awesome; thank you! And Jean, the patient and HCP quotes you pulled were amazing; thank you, and we miss you.

Speaking of missing people: Madeline Good, thank you for the great early cover design, reading carefully through many early drafts, and your always on-point comments. And Alexandra Quintero, for picking up where Madeline left off and making sure we did not miss a beat in getting this book to market. You both are awesome!

Gary White, thank you for the detailed review of an early version of this book. Your ideas on underserved patient populations and how it relates to CX was brilliant! This book is so much better because of your thoughtful and detailed feedback. Thank you so much!

Jeff Kohl, when you commented that you were expecting a story to grab you in Chapter 1, it hit me that this was a major gap in the book. You were right, and it changed Chapter 1 completely (for the better). Thank you for this insight among many you provided!

I am so grateful to Trancelerate for allowing us to include the Study Participant Feedback Questionnaire (the "SPFQ") in this book. It made the clinical trial section of the book so much better! The Study Participate Feedback Questionnaire is copyrighted with Trancelerate BioPharma Inc. and is used with permission.

I also want to thank PeopleMetrics's pharmaceutical and biotechnology clients who made the content in the book possible and provided feedback on an early draft. It's an honor to work with all of you and be a small part of helping you break the mold and truly become customer-centric. In all the conversations I had with you based on an early draft of this book, you all pointed out the regulatory constraints pharma is under and that it was important to acknowledge this early in the book. You were all 100 percent correct, and the final version reflects that. Thank you so much!

Finally, I would like to thank my two sons, Ben and Henry, who watched me work on this book for over a year and listened to me talk about it endlessly. Everything I do, I do for you. I love you both.

ABOUT THE AUTHOR

SEAN MCDADE has been helping companies optimize customer experiences for over twenty years. He is the founder, CEO, and visionary of PeopleMetrics, a leading provider of experience management software and advisory services. Sean has worked with leading pharmaceutical and biotechnology companies such as AstraZeneca, Sanofi, and Novartis. He has created PeopleMetrics pharma CX solutions, including the Patient Hierarchy of Needs framework for patient support services that is featured in this book. Sean's first book, *Listen or Die: 40 Lessons that Turn Customer Feedback into Gold*, was an Amazon bestseller. He holds a PhD in Business Administration and Marketing Science from Temple University and has published eight articles in peer-reviewed scholarly journals. A recipient of Philadelphia Business Journal's 40 Under 40 award, Sean is also an active angel investor in the Philadelphia region. Sean resides in Philadelphia and spends as much time as possible in Brigantine, NJ, during the summer with his two sons, Ben and Henry.

CPSIA information can be obtained
at www.ICGtesting.com
Printed in the USA
BVHW030543151121
621608BV00002B/5

9 781544 525594